MW01595014

THE TOP TEN STINKING

LIES FROM THE PULPIT

By Rick White

Foreword by Loel Passe

This book is dedicated to
Jude Miles White, my grandson.
Grandpa loves you so much, Jude.
I know you will grow up to be a person of grace,
and I cannot wait to watch.

Contents

Foreword

The book you are about to read is a bold and timely exposé on a very touchy subject - **stinking lies told from the pulpit**. Fasten your seatbelts! This is going to be an eye-opening journey! To say it will be controversial would be an understatement. You are about to discover some shocking revelations about ten commonly accepted Biblical *myths*.

First, let me say that it is certainly a great privilege to work with such an honest servant of God as Pastor Rick White and to be asked to write the foreword to this highly controversial book. Not only have I known Pastor Rick for three decades, but I have been involved with him in Christian ministries and music for many of those years. We are the closest of friends and brothers in the Lord. He is a man of honor and integrity who speaks the truth, no matter how popular or unpopular it may be. This book is no exception. In fact, it touches areas and questionable doctrinal positions that others have been afraid to address or even discuss, precisely because they are so controversial.

Pastor Rick is undoubtedly qualified to write this book about exposing the most common LIES told from the pulpits of Christian churches around the world. It is especially the modern church, right here in America, that is the worst offender. For many of our years working together,

Rick and I were deeply involved in the area of *apologetics* - which is the Biblical defense of the faith. There has never been a time when this new, unabashed exposé is more needed than today, when many of the very core doctrines of the faith, when many of the basic fundamental truths about Christianity, are being distorted and put in the form of enticing lies. They are told from the pulpit by thousands of pastors and teachers every week.

I can assure you that this book will rock you to the core. There will be at least two or three of these false beliefs that you took for granted as true! It even surprised me. I, like so many Christians, just *absorbed* some of these untruths over the years. When you hear them over and over for so long, they just get into you. In many cases, they start to sound correct to our ears after hearing them repeated over and over again.

Jesus said:

"You will know the truth and the truth will make you free."[1]

That is why it is important to know the deceptive and destructive nature of these lies, which will only undermine your faith and walk with Jesus. You can be free from them!

Some people will say that this book is just *nit-picking*, over-emphasizing the differences and varying positions within Christian dogma. But that is not the case. Pastor Rick is not saying that all of the people teaching these errors are not genuine Christians or not our brothers in the faith. Let's be very clear here. There is a difference between aberrant teaching and outright heresy. But I must say, some of these lies are so insidious and deceptive that they border on actual heresy itself because they attack the very person and work of the Lord Jesus Christ! Even more seriously, some of them are actually **another gospel**. You may get offended because some of your favorite Bible teachers may be the very ones who are spewing out these lies. As believers, we should all love TRUTH more than any ministry or even our favorite Bible teacher.

So, brace yourself! Are you ready? This book will undoubtedly challenge you. It will challenge some of the crucial beliefs that many of us still hold or have held since becoming a Christian. False teaching can only harm you! Scripture after Scripture will be given in this book to liberate you from these common lies, which sound so truthful and right, **on the surface**. I say, "So be it! Let the truth be told."

Thank you for writing another eye-opening book, my friend.

Loel Passe

Introduction

I have been involved in ministry for almost four decades, preaching from the pulpit a lot of that time. I have attended and ministered in many kinds of churches, and I have heard many lies from the pulpit. Unfortunately, I have even taught some.

In this book, we will expose these severe instances of false doctrine and most likely stir up a little controversy. But hey, so did Jesus. So, I am not worried about that.

Here are the Top 10 Stinking Lies from the Pulpit:

1. Your salvation is dependent upon you.

The majority of American churches preach this.

2. You can lose your salvation.

We know that approximately fifty percent of Christians believe this lie.

3. God gets mad at Christians.

Almost everyone teaches this. I cannot wait for you to read this chapter. It really could change your life.

4. God gets disappointed with Christians.

It may be a shock to you that this is a lie, but it is.

5. The Holy Spirit convicts Christians of sin.

Before you close this book and say I am a heretic, wait until chapter five, so I can prove to you that this is not scriptural.

6. Repentance is YOUR part of the salvation equation.

You may not think this is a lie, but it is a subtle one.

7. A Loving God would not punish people for eternity.

This lie says that there cannot be a hell because God is love, and therefore, He could not put people in hell for eternity.

8. You have to be willing to give up everything in order to be saved.

This lie is taught by possibly the most famous evangelical teacher out there today.

9. Christians can become so holy in this life that they no longer sin.

Yes, sinless perfection is a lie.

10. It is not God's will for Christians to suffer.

Only in America and other rich countries could this lie flourish.

These doctrines are stinking lies because they do not present the gospel nor Jesus accurately from a Biblical perspective. Now, before we go on, I want to be clear that I do not believe I have one hundred percent accurate doctrine. We are all in school, so to speak, learning more and more as we grow in the Lord. But that does not remove from me the responsibility to point out false doctrine and correct it to the best of my ability. 2 Timothy 4:2 instructs me to:

Preach the word of God. Be prepared, whether the time is favorable or not. Patiently correct, rebuke, and encourage your people with good teaching.[2]

So, that is the spirit of this book - correction. However, I am also a comedian, and I can be very snarky at times. If you are easily offended, you may not last through too many chapters, but I hope you do. Once you see that these teachings are not true, you will be set free. Why? Not because I am a great theologian, a great writer, or even a great Christian. You will be set free because that is what the truth of Scripture does. It is my prayer that this book will show you that God's grace is more amazing than you ever thought possible. I hope that, by the end of this book, you say to yourself, "Wow, this sounds too good to be true." Because that is how you should feel when you understand the unmitigated grace of God. I pray He blesses you through this book.

Thanks for reading.

Rick

Lie #1 Your Salvation Is Dependent on You

This is our first lie. This lie says that you must meet many conditions to be saved and continue to meet them to maintain your salvation. What does that sound like from the pulpit? This lie is preached with statements such as:

- Keep short accounts with God.
- Unconfessed sin can keep a Christian from heaven.
- You must be willing to give up everything for God.
- It is healthy to doubt your salvation.
- It is time for you to make a decision for Christ.

Have you heard those things? I certainly have. Guess what! Every one of them is unscriptural. I know that may sound shocking, so allow me the chance to prove my assertion scripturally. First, let's look at John 15:16:

You didn't choose me. I chose you. I appointed you to go and produce lasting fruit, so that the Father will give you whatever you ask for, using my name.[3]

Here, Jesus is saying that we did not become His disciples due to an act of our will. Instead, it was an act of Jesus's will. That is very clear in this verse. How could anyone argue with that? Well, some legalists argue that He was only talking to his disciples here. Is that true? Well, let's see if there are other Scriptures that support our interpretation.

Paul says in Romans 9:18:

So you see, God chooses to show mercy to some, and he chooses to harden the hearts of others, so they refuse to listen.[4]

There are many teachers out there who want to take their black Bible highlighter to Romans 9:18. Why? Because it takes you and me out of the picture. God hardens the hearts of some so that they will refuse to listen and refuse to receive His gift.

Now, before you get upset with me, remember, I did not write this verse - the Apostle Paul did. Paul says that God chooses to have mercy on some and to essentially cast others away. I know that might not fit in well with 21st century American Evangelical Christianity. However, as you will see in this book, it is clearly taught in Scripture.

We are involved in a spiritual war on Earth between good and evil. And guess what! Not everyone is picked by God to be on the winning side. That seems very unfair to us humans. Paul anticipated the unfairness complaint and answered it in such a way as to put us in our place. We think we can tell God what is fair and what is not. That is patently absurd. Paul's answer to our accusation of unfairness with God is found in Romans 9:20-24:

No, don't say that. Who are you, a mere human being, to argue with God? Should the thing that was created say to the one who created it, "Why have you made me like this?" When a potter makes jars out of clay, doesn't he have a right to use the same lump of clay to make one jar for decoration and another to throw garbage into? In the same way, even though God has the right to show his anger and his power, he is very patient with those on whom his anger falls, who are destined for destruction. He does this to make the riches of his glory shine even brighter on those to whom he shows mercy, who were prepared in advance for glory. And we are among those whom he selected, both from the Jews and from the Gentiles.[5]

We were prepared in advance for glory. *In advance* means we are **already** prepared for glory. The Bible often talks about the church being God's elect. It is God who chooses us, and it is not based on anything in us.

The Bible also has a lot to say about covenants. We know about the Old Covenant and the New Covenant. In Biblical times, covenants were a big part of normal life. They were used for marriage, business partnerships, and other important agreements. Often, they ratified political agreements between nations.

The process for sealing the covenant was rather gruesome. They would cut several animals in half and put the halves on either side of a pathway. Those who were making the covenant would walk together down that pathway. This signified that both parties were serious about their part in the covenant. Through the ceremony, the parties were stating that what was done to the animals should be done to them if they break the covenant. Then, after the ceremony, they would cook the animals and have a feast. That is the way covenants were made in the Old Testament. Now, why do I bring that up? Well, let's take a look at the covenant that God made with Abraham.

He tells Abraham that his children are going to be as many as the stars in heaven and that they will possess the Promised Land. Abraham answers that what God said would be impossible. He reminds the Lord that he and Sarah are very old. Abraham asks the Lord how he could be certain that God's promise would come to pass. God's answer is to make a covenant with Abraham. He has Abraham set up everything for the ceremony, which includes killing and bisecting the animals. But then, after everything is set up, God does something very surprising. Genesis 15:17 says:

After the sun went down and darkness fell, Abram saw a smoking firepot and a flaming torch pass between the halves of the carcasses.[6]

Notice that, in this covenant, only one party walked between the halves of the carcasses. The firepot and the torch both represent God. He could have easily told Abraham to walk with Him down the pathway, but He did not. What is the significance of that? It is this. God made a covenant with Himself. He did not make a covenant with fallen, sinful Abraham, in which Abraham had to live up to his part.

God ratified the covenant alone and sealed it with the shedding of blood. What was Abraham's involvement? Well, he was involved in the setup, but definitely not in the covenant ceremony itself, nor did he make any promise to God.

God knew that Abraham could not play a part in the covenant. The covenant could not depend on Abraham's obedience. If that is how God instituted the Old Covenant, how could the New Covenant of grace be **more** dependent on man's effort than the Old Covenant was? I encourage you to read Genesis 15 to get an appreciation for the scene. God is teaching us about His grace, even by the way He instituted the Old Covenant.

As I am sure you remember, Jesus said, "It is finished." just before He died. What did He mean? What was finished? Have you ever wondered about that? Was He just saying, "I am at the end. I do not have any more strength, so I am going to die now"? Is that what He meant? Before I started studying Scripture, that is what I thought Jesus meant. But that is not correct. The Greek word translated "it is finished" is *tetelestai*. This word is used in accounting, and it means *paid in full*. If you made the last payment on your Corvette, the car dealership could stamp your invoice with the word *tetelestai*. The loan is finished - paid in full. The books have been reconciled.

So, here is a question. If you had something to do with your salvation, why did Jesus not say, "It is almost finished. I did My part. The rest is up to you."?

Let's look at it another way. We believe that Jesus atoned for sins on the cross, right? It is difficult to find a Christian who would disagree with that. Well, what does atonement mean? It means paid for, dealt with, reconciled, covered, finished, removed, and done.

Now, how can it be that two thousand years ago, long before I was born, Jesus paid for some of my sins but not others? Did He intend to atone for only my pre-Christian sins? After I became born-again, do I have to keep short accounts with God? In light of all we have discussed so far, does that make any sense to you? We must be careful not to trample underfoot the grace of God. Jesus paid for all of the sins of his church, past - present - and future.

If you have been around the church long enough, you have heard these legalistic concepts like *keep short accounts*, etc. Here is the problem with that bad theology. You cannot live up. You cannot make yourself worthy. You cannot help get yourself saved from hell. Jesus paid it all! There is no invoice on your account that is past due. There are no installment payments. There is nothing outstanding on your account. You are bankrupt, anyway. If there were payments you needed to make, you would not be able to afford even the first one. Once you and I realize this about ourselves, we are not far from the kingdom.

Maybe we can take *some* of the credit. We at least realized our bankruptcy on our own and discovered that we needed God, right? Nope. For us to even realize our condition before God, the Holy Spirit had to move first and open our eyes. We, quite literally, bring nothing to the table.

If you do not have a relationship with the Lord, I hope these words are being used by the Holy Spirit right now in your heart. I cannot convince you of anything. But what I can do is give you some things to think about. Why not take this opportunity to ask God if this is correct? Ask God to show you, in your heart and in Scripture, whether what you have read so far is true. You may be surprised. God will show you the truth. You will live in a new kind of freedom. You will be free to receive from God His amazing gift of grace. You will be able to admit that you do not deserve His grace. But, as we have shown, your worthiness is not even on the table. It is not part of this covenant. God walks the pathway alone, sealing the covenant with the blood of His Son, Jesus.

When, as a Christian, you realize you did nothing to earn salvation, you stop trying to pay God for it. You are not supposed to pay for gifts. You are supposed to receive them and say, "Thank You!" Instead of worrying about paying for the gift, you grow in love for the Gift Giver. You want to get to know Him better. His love draws you into a deeper relationship with Him.

Why does my little grandson do whatever he can to get the attention of his mom and dad, and even his grandma and grandpa, when he is hungry? Because he knows that, if he just gets with one of us, we are going to make a bottle and meet his need. He does not have to make the bottle. He does not have to do anything. He just lets us know of his need and then trusts.

Religion wants you to trust in your part of the deal. *"God has done his part. You have to do your part."* This is a lie, a stinking lie told from many pulpits. Why does this matter? Because if salvation depends on anything in you or in me, we are doomed.

On Earth, we like to compare people. There are good people and bad people. Mother Theresa was good. Adolph

Hitler was bad. But that is not completely accurate. God is light years away from us in the holiness department. From the perspective of God's holiness, we are all the same. We are all bankrupt before Him.

Realizing this, we throw ourselves at His mercy, and we say,

"I am empty. I bring nothing to You. But if You'll have me, please come into my heart."

God answers that prayer, and we are never the same. But even realizing that we need His mercy and grace takes the work of the Holy Spirit. No one can even pray for salvation unless God has already begun to work in their heart. So, stand against the lie that you have contributed to this salvation equation. Fess up that you are bankrupt. When someone tells you that you have to do your part, explain that there is no part of your redemption that you can accomplish. It is all a gift.

Let's look at one of my favorite Scriptures, to even further drive this message home. Ephesians 2:8-9 says:

God saved you by his grace when you believed. And you can't take credit for this; it is a gift from God. Salvation is not a reward for the good things we have done, so none of us can boast about it. [7]

This verse says that you have been saved by grace, which is defined as *undeserved kindness*. It takes one thing on your part: faith. But even that faith is not from you. It is the gift of God, not as a result of anything you could possibly do because you would boast. God decided to set things up this way because if you had something to do with this transaction, you would take credit for it. You would say,

"I wasn't quite as bad as those people who didn't get saved. At least I figured it out. At least I weighed the pros and cons in my mind and made a decision for Christ."

But that is not what happens. The old hymn happens - "He Touched Me." The Holy Spirit touches your heart, your eyes are opened, and you say,

"Lord, I am a sinner. I need your grace."

You are not the first mover. God is. You bring nothing to the table.

Lie # 1 is: "Your salvation is dependent on you." We have nine more lies coming in the following chapters. Recognizing these lies will set you free. We will probably piss off some religious people (I probably just did with that sentence). That is OK. If you have seen any of our literature, you know that we are just not interested in legalistic BS anymore. And one of the most legalistic concepts out there is:

God did His part. Make sure you do your part.

We are calling BS. Salvation is of grace. Otherwise, we are all in big trouble.

As I close this chapter, I want to give you an opportunity to receive this salvation if you are not sure that you are a Christian. And, if you are not sure, that probably means you are not a Christian, in the Biblical sense. It either means that or someone has fed you these legalistic lies, and you have started to believe them. Either way, I want to pray for you right now.

Lord, I pray for those reading this right now, whether they have been in Your church for decades, or they have stayed away from Christians and churches in general because they just thought it was all hypocrisy. Lord, I pray that the truth that salvation is a free gift would be revealed by Your Holy Spirit. I cannot convince anyone. All the arguments in the world cannot convince anyone. But I pray that, by Your Spirit, people will see that You are the Great Giver of eternal life. I pray that You will move on people's hearts so that they will put their trust in Your finished work.

In Your name, Jesus, I pray. Amen.

Lie #2 You Can Lose Your Salvation

Eternal security, or as John Calvin called it, the perseverance of the saints, is the doctrine that once a person becomes born-again, they can never become un-born-again. Detractors call it "once saved, always saved (OSAS)." They may think that name is derogatory, but I do not. I proudly believe in OSAS.

Now, this subject has been a matter of debate and division since the Reformation and even before. In this chapter, I will give you the verses that prove OSAS, and I will expose the misinterpretation of a verse that many people attempt to use to disprove it.

But before I do, let's talk about why this topic matters. Actually, it more than matters. A proper understanding of this doctrine is indispensable to living a victorious Christian life. If you don't understand this, you will live a life of worry, defeat, and legalism. This doctrine is one of the keys to throwing away legalism forever.

Now, I want to start with John 6:35-40. This Scripture almost nails the door shut on whether you can lose your salvation.

Jesus replied, I am the bread of life. Whoever comes to me will never be hungry again. Whoever believes in me will never be thirsty. But you haven't believed in me even though you have seen me. However, those the Father has given me will come to me and I will never reject them. For

I have come down from heaven to do the will of God who sent me, not to do my own will. And this is the will of God, that I should not lose even one of all those he has given me, but that I should raise them up on the last day. For it is my Father's will that all who see his Son and believe in him should have eternal life. I will raise them up at the last day.[8]

Let's take this apart. The first thing I want you to notice is the word **never**, which is in these verses several times.

*I am the bread of life. Whoever comes to me will **never** be hungry again.*

You know what never means. It means that something is not ever going to happen. Now, does the above mean that Christians are never hungry in their stomachs? No, that is not what Jesus is talking about. Jesus says that He is "The Bread of Life." He is talking about spiritual life - the hunger to know that you are loved, accepted, and forgiven by God - the thirst to know that the Creator of the Universe accepts you and loves you. Jesus says, if you come to Him, you will **never** have that thirst again. Notice, He does not say,

"You will not be thirsty again until you mess up and deny Jesus or sin in some way. After that, you will be thirsty again."

The next *never* is:

*he who believes in me will **never** be thirsty,*

Again, this is not talking about physical thirst but thirst for the water of life. He even reiterates this after His resurrection, in Revelation 22:17:

The Spirit and the bride say, "Come." Let anyone who hears this say, "Come." Let anyone who is thirsty come. Let anyone who desires drink freely from the water of life.[9]

We will **never** have an unquenched thirst for the water of life again if we are saved.

Let's go back to John 6. There is another ***never*** in verse 37:

*However, those the father has given me will come to me and I will **never** reject them.*

This is such a clear defense of eternal security. Jesus is explaining a process - the *ordo salutis* - which is a Latin theological term meaning *order of salvation.* Here is the order Jesus articulates:

1. The Father gives people to Jesus.
2. All that the Father gives to Jesus WILL come to Him.
3. Jesus will not lose **even one** of those that the Father gives to Him.
4. Jesus will raise every one of them up to eternal life.

If you come to Jesus, you've been given to Jesus by God. He will never, ever reject you. He will never distance Himself from you because of your sin kooties.

These verses say that Jesus will not lose a single Christian, and just in case we didn't get that, He adds that all Christians will be raised up on the last day.

Now, that is not talking about the general resurrection, where the unregenerate are resurrected. We know that because verse 40 says:

For it is my Father's will that all who see his Son and believe in him should have eternal life.

Therefore, this must be the resurrection of Christians. It is very difficult to squeeze into these verses the interpretation that Christians can lose their salvation. If that is true, then Jesus lied here. At the very least, He lied by omission. He should have at least stated a disclaimer:

Oh, by the way, if you walk away from God, THEN He will abandon you. THEN He will reject you.

Another verse that clearly demonstrates eternal security is John 10:27-29:

*My sheep listen to my voice; I know them, and they follow me. I give them eternal life, and they will **never** perish. No one can snatch them away from me, for my Father has given them to me, and he is more powerful than anyone else. No one can snatch them from the Father's hand.[10]*

There is that word again.

*and they will **never** perish.*

No one can snatch a Christian out of God's hands. God is more powerful than anyone else.

Sometimes, when Jesus was speaking, His purpose was to show how difficult it is to be acceptable to God based on the law. When He told the rich young ruler to sell everything, He was not expecting the rich young ruler to obey. Jesus knew he could not obey. That was the whole point. He raised the bar to show this man, who thought he was pretty good, that his heart was still wicked (more on this subject is coming in Lie #8). Often, Jesus's purpose is to show that we are hopeless without Him. But at other times, when He talks as He does in John 6:35-40, He has another purpose. And that purpose is the gospel.

When Jesus says that no one can snatch a Christian from the Father's hand, no one includes the Christian who is *in* the Father's hand. No one includes you. You cannot snatch yourself out of the Father's hand.

But what about free will? That is the objection often heard. Listen, unregenerate humans have a very limited free will. Those who preach that free will is sovereign say the following:

- God has done everything, and now it is up to you to choose.
- If you do not choose the right thing, you have undone all of God's work.
- God really wanted you, but you didn't get it. So, God does not get what He wants.

We do not have that kind of unlimited free will. If you want to read more about this, I highly recommend you check out Martin Luther's book called "The Bondage of the Will." In that book, Luther teaches that we do have limited freedom of will. I can decide to go to the store. I can decide to have chicken or beef for dinner. But our will has a boundary around it.

Here is an analogy that may help. A dog is free to bark. A dog is not free to meow. Even if he wants to, he cannot because he is not that kind of creature. He is not free to be something other than what he is. Now, how does that apply to what we are talking about? Here is how. The Bible says in Romans 3:10:

As the Scriptures say, "No one is righteous— not even one.[11]

1 Corinthians 2:14 states:

But people who aren't spiritual can't receive these truths from God's Spirit. It all sounds foolish to them and they can't understand it, for only those who are spiritual can understand what the Spirit means.[12]

Without God's intervention, you cannot even understand the gospel. You, in your natural being, are not free to make a decision for Christ. Defining salvation as "making a decision for Christ" is horrible theology. You are not free to choose Christ, not when Scripture says that your thoughts are only evil continually. There is none righteous - no, not one.

Here is an interesting question. Does it please God if you accept Jesus? Of course, it does. But, dead, unsaved people cannot please God. We are dead to Him. So, an unregenerate person cannot make a decision for Christ.

Take the story of Lazarus as an example. He died and was in a tomb for three days. His sisters, Martha and Mary, told the Lord not to go into the tomb. They said there would be a foul odor. This shows that they knew he was dead. There is no doubt that he was dead. When Jesus said Lazarus was only sleeping, he did not literally mean Lazarus was just taking a nap. He meant that dying, once we are in Christ, seems like sleep from the earthly perspective, but we are not gone. Then He called out, "Lazarus, come forth!" Here is something to consider. Did Lazarus have to be willing to come forth? Did Lazarus have to make a choice to obey Jesus's command? The answer is no. Lazarus could not make a choice. Dead people do not make choices. The same is true of spiritually dead people. Spiritually dead people cannot make spiritually positive choices. An unregenerate person cannot will himself to be regenerate. We have a certain, very limited kind of free will.

Now, that does not mean that we do not sin after we are regenerated. Of course, we do. What it means is that your salvation did not come based on what you do, and therefore it cannot be lost based on what you do. You did nothing to earn it, so you can do nothing to lose it.

You did not accept the gospel by making a decision in your brain. The Spirit of God was already working in you, and all of a sudden, your mind and your eyes were opened. That is how you accepted the gospel. Now, if you accepted the gospel and got saved, but it was not based on your works, how possibly could you lose it based on your works?

Paul addresses this very question in Galatians 3:1-5:

Oh, foolish Galatians! Who has cast an evil spell on you? For the meaning of Jesus Christ's death was made as clear to you as if you had seen a picture of his death on the cross. Let me ask you this one question: Did you receive the Holy Spirit by obeying the law of Moses? Of course not! You received the Spirit because you believed the message you heard about Christ. How foolish can you be? After starting your new lives in the Spirit, why are you now trying to become perfect by your own human effort? Have you experienced so much for nothing? Surely it was not in vain, was it?

I ask you again, does God give you the Holy Spirit and work miracles among you because you obey the law? Of course not! It is because you believe the message you heard about Christ.[13]

Paul hits this heresy hard in Galatians. He even suggests that if they are trusting in their obedience, they may not be saved. Verse 4 says:

Have you experienced so much for nothing? Surely it was not in vain, was it?[14]

He is suggesting here that if the Galatians moved from grace-based salvation to works-based salvation, maybe they were never saved. Maybe all of his work there was in vain. This is how serious it is to trust in your obedience.

Can anything ever separate us from Christ's love? Paul answers this clearly in Romans 8:35-40:

Can anything ever separate us from Christ's love? Does it mean he no longer loves us if we have trouble or calamity, or are persecuted, or hungry, or destitute, or in danger, or threatened with death? (As the Scriptures say, "For your sake we are killed every day; we are being slaughtered like sheep.") No, despite all these things, overwhelming victory is ours through Christ, who loved us.

And I am convinced that nothing can ever separate us from God's love. Neither death nor life, neither angels nor demons, neither our fears for today nor our worries about tomorrow—not even the powers of hell can separate us from God's love. No power in the sky above or in the earth below—indeed, nothing in all creation will ever be able to separate us from the love of God that is revealed in Christ Jesus our Lord.[15]

Nothing in all of creation can separate us from the love of God that is revealed in Jesus. Are you part of *all of creation?* Of course, you are. Therefore, you cannot separate yourself from the love of God.

In Philippians 1:6, Paul tells us that he is **certain** that God will finish the work He started in us.

And I am certain that God, who began the good work within you, will continue his work until it is finally finished on the day when Christ Jesus returns.[16]

We all need to remember this verse when the fiery darts of legalism come. Did Paul say, "*and I am certain that **you** will finish **your** work so that you will be acceptable to God*"?

Did he say, "*I am certain that if you are a Christian, you will learn how to behave.*"?

Nope. Paul said that he was certain that God, Who began a good work within you, will continue His work until it is finally finished on the day when Christ returns. God is going to be working on us forever. But it is His work. It is not our work.

We have a lot of verses in this chapter, and there are still more to come. Why? Because there are people out there that are going to try to rob you of your assurance of salvation. And there may be people reading this who have already been robbed of that, who think, "I am no longer sure that I am going to heaven." Yet, there are multitudes of verses that are written to give us confidence and assurance. Here is another verse that puts another nail in the door of works-based salvation. 1 Peter 1:4-5 states:

and we have a priceless inheritance—an inheritance that is kept in heaven for you, pure and undefiled, beyond the reach of change and decay. And through your faith, God is protecting you by his power until you receive this salvation, which is ready to be revealed on the last day for all to see.[17]

There are some very significant truths in that verse. It says that our inheritance, which is salvation, is kept in heaven, pure and undefiled, beyond the reach of change or decay.

Do you think you can change your eternal destiny? These verses say that you cannot. They say that your salvation is being kept safe as an inheritance for you in heaven. No one can tamper with it. It is being kept safe from what? It is protected from change and decay. I am changing all the time. I am decaying. We are all dying. We are all getting a little bit closer to the end of our lives with every passing day.

The longer I am a Christian, the more I see the weakness and the sinfulness of my own flesh. I do not feel like I am getting better. But my fickle feelings do not matter because my salvation is protected. It is being kept for me, safe and secure by God Himself, in heaven. Do you think you can mess that up? Do you think you can reach under the protection of God and destroy your inheritance? Are you more powerful than God, Who is protecting your salvation? I think we know the answer. Losing your salvation is a lie from the pit of hell.

There is a verse that people use all the time to attempt to prove that Christians can lose salvation. Let's see if their point makes sense. Hebrews 6:4-6 says:

For it is impossible to bring back to repentance those who were once enlightened—those who have experienced the good things of heaven and shared in the Holy Spirit, who have tasted the goodness of the word of God and the power of the age to come— and who then turn away from God. It is impossible to bring such people back to repentance; by rejecting the Son of God, they themselves are nailing him to the cross once again and holding him up to public shame.[18]

This verse is used to say that if you embraced Christianity, repented, shared in the Holy Spirit, tasted the goodness of heaven, and then turned away from God, it is impossible to go back to repentance.

Let's stop right there for a bit. First of all, those who interpret this verse to say it is talking about losing your salvation must move from our position of *once saved, always saved* to *once saved, then lost, always lost.* If this is talking about Christians losing their salvation, then they are worse off than an unsaved person because an unsaved person can repent. According to this interpretation, these verses say Christians cannot repent after falling away.

If the above interpretation of Hebrews 6 is correct, does it jive with the overarching message of Scripture? We have quoted numerous verses so far in this book. And none of them agree with this interpretation. Here is a valuable hermeneutic principle. If you have multiple verses that are in agreement and one that seems to contradict those verses, you are not interpreting that one verse correctly. So, either this interpretation is incorrect, or God is confusing. Yet, the Bible says that God is not the author of confusion.

So, what does this verse actually mean? Well, there are two opinions out there, and I will give you both of them. And I am kind of 50/50 on which interpretation I support. I lean toward the first one.

Interpretation 1:

If it were ever possible for a saved person to lose their salvation, then it would be all over. We cannot go back to repentance. Christ died once and said, "It is finished." So, if a Christian needed to be saved again, there is no longer a sacrifice being offered for them. It was offered once. The author of Hebrews is saying that if Christians can lose their salvation, Christ would have to be continually sacrificed.

So, according to this interpretation, this verse actually teaches the opposite of what legalists say it does. It is teaching the impossibility of losing salvation. We do not re-crucify Jesus every time a person sins.

Interpretation 2:

This interpretation says that Christians will continue to sin, and when they do, they do not need to go back to the beginning. It may look like they have lost their salvation, but it is impossible to get re-saved. They are already saved.

Again, I like both of those interpretations. They both agree with the consistent message of Scripture. But what this does NOT say is that once you are saved, you can lose your salvation.

And what it definitely does not say is that you can go up and down like a roller coaster. Yet, most people who are against eternal security try to make this verse say that very thing. If that is what this verse means, you can never get it back. If this verse is talking about losing your salvation, then you must preach *once lost, always lost*, and we know that cannot be what this means.

Matthew 7:21-23 gives us more insight into this topic. Jesus said:

"Not everyone who calls out to me, 'Lord! Lord!' will enter the Kingdom of Heaven. Only those who actually do the will of my Father in heaven will enter. On judgment day many will say to me, 'Lord! Lord! We prophesied in your name and cast out demons in your name and performed many

miracles in your name.' But I will reply, 'I never knew you. Get away from me, you who break God's laws.'[19]

Some people think that these verses are discussing people who genuinely got saved. But, if we look closer, we will see that this is not talking about Christians.

First, it says only those who actually do the will of the Father in heaven will enter. Legalists use this verse to say you must obey everything perfectly. But what is the will of the Father? In John 6:40, Jesus said:

For it is my Father's will that all who see his Son and believe in him should have eternal life. I will raise them up at the last day.[20]

We can also tell that this verse is not talking about salvation by works because Jesus tells us here of people that have done many mighty works for God. They prophesied. They cast out demons. They performed miracles. And what does He say? "I never knew you." There's that word again. **Never**. Jesus is saying, "Ok. You did some things in My name, but you **never** had a *relationship* with Me. You did not get saved." In light of that, what He says next makes sense.

Get away from me, you who break God's laws.[21]

Jesus would never say that to someone whose sins were atoned for on the cross. If you are a Christian, Jesus will never say to you, "Get away from me." Why? Because our breaking of God's laws has been covered and paid for, and we have been declared not guilty. You who break God's laws must refer to people who did not get saved. There is no place in the Bible that talks about Christians losing their salvation.

There is another great analogy of the permanence of our salvation in Psalm 103:12:

He has removed our sins as far from us as the east is from the west.[22]

Now, here is an interesting thought. In Biblical times, they did not know that the world was round. As is often the case with Scripture, scientific facts are stated by the inspiration of the Holy Spirit long before they have been discovered by humans.

If you start going south from the north pole and continue south, once you get around the south pole, you will be going north again. So south meets north, and north meets south at both poles.

But if you start going around the equator heading east, you will never start going west. East never meets west. And that is how far away God has removed our sins from us. Shame on anyone who tries to put us under the guilt of our sins. God has removed them as far as the east is from the west, which is an infinite distance.

I believe we have shown that the statement that a Christian can lose their salvation is a lie. In fact, it is a stinking lie. Well, who would tell you this lie? I think our three enemies love to tell this whopper.

Our three enemies are the world, the flesh, and the devil. The world means the anti-God system of this planet and all of those who do not have a relationship with Jesus. But these are not all obviously blatant heathens. Some are wolves in sheep's clothing. Pastors who teach false doctrine with regards to soteriology - how one gets saved - are part of the world too.

The flesh, your fallen nature, will condemn you as well. The voices in your head and your own sense of wanting to be good will condemn you every time you mess up.

The devil is called the accuser of the brethren. Of course, he is going to tell you this lie. He says things like,

"Listen, at one time, you loved God, but you've really lost your salvation. You're just like everyone else, and you're going to hell."

That is a lie from the pit of hell. If God ever moved in, if you ever open the door when He knocked on your heart, He never leaves. That is the promise of Christianity.

So, Christian, this is the good news that you should celebrate every day. Never means never, and you are never going to lose your salvation. And if you are not a Christian, have I got a deal for you! This is a deal you must not pass up. Surrender to Jesus. Admit that you are a sinner and that you need Him to save you. You will receive a gift that you would never, ever be able to earn. You do not earn gifts anyway. That is not the way gifts work.

I am going to leave you with the story of Jim Elliott. Jim was a missionary who was murdered before he was 40. Elliott loved the Lord and was very active in ministry. He always wanted to go to Ecuador to evangelize and be a missionary.

He eventually got his wish and, after several years of work, he was making some inroads with a tribe there. Members of the tribe set Jim up to meet some of the tribal leaders. When the meeting happened, they murdered Jim. I tell you this story because Mr. Elliott is the originator of the phrase:

He is no fool who gives what he cannot keep to gain what he cannot lose.

When you come to Christ, what are you giving? You are just giving up. You are saying, "Lord, I need help." You are giving up control of your life. You are saying, Lord, you take over. Listen, you cannot keep it anyway. If you are ten years old, you have sixty to eighty years left. Only a fool would hang on to their temporary independence and assert that they are the master of their own fate. Time will prove to the fool that they are the master of nothing.

Why would anyone cling to this life, which they will inevitably lose, and at the same time reject eternal life, which they could never lose?

Salvation is a free gift. Jim Elliott saw it, and he ended up giving his life for it. He knew he could lose everything, but he was not going to lose his salvation.

If you have been regenerated - born-again - you will be in heaven. The deal is done, and it is not dependent on you. Remember, just like He did with Abraham, God made this New Covenant with Himself.

Lie #3 God Gets Mad At Christians

Then I heard a mighty voice from the Temple say to the seven angels, "Go your ways and pour out on the earth the seven bowls containing God's wrath." Revelation 16:1[23]

Wrath is defined as:

vengeance or punishment as the consequence of anger

God has anger for unbelieving sinners. He also loves them. Because of that, His anger is restrained at the moment. However, the future displays of His wrath will be terribly devastating and much worse than anything the human race has ever seen. Consider some of the end times catastrophes that are promised in Revelation chapter 16:

1. People will break out with malignant sores. (verse 2)
2. The sea will become like blood, and all living things in it will die. (verse 3)
3. Rivers and springs will become like blood. (verse 4)
4. The sun will scorch everyone. (verse 8)
5. Pain and sores will cause people to grind their teeth in anguish. (verse 10)
6. The Euphrates River will dry up. (verse 12)
7. Evil spirits that look like frogs will assemble the rulers of the world to fight against the Lord at the battle of Armageddon. (verses 13-16)

8. The worst earthquake in the history of the world will occur. Islands will disappear, and mountains will be leveled. (verses 17-20)
9. Seventy-five-pound hailstones will fall on people. (verse 21)

The wrath of God is indeed a terrible and devastating thing. God is justified in this display of vengeance. He is Holy, and we are not. He cannot let sin go unpunished.

But, will any of this wrath be visited upon Christians? To answer this question, we must understand the concept of *substitutionary atonement*. Substitutionary atonement is the doctrine that Jesus atoned or paid for others' sins when He died in their place as their substitute. The anger of God, anger severe enough to be demonstrated in the above acts, was poured out on Jesus. He deserved none of it, but He willingly took this wrath on behalf of those that belong to Him. This is the classic, historic, Biblical doctrine of substitutionary atonement. If this doctrine is accurate, then God's anger against Christians has been poured out on Jesus. There is none left for us. Consider the following verses.

2 Corinthians 5:21:

For God made Christ, who never sinned, to be the offering for our sin, so that we could be made right with God through Christ.[24]

1 Peter 2:24:

He personally carried our sins in his body on the cross so that we can be dead to sin and live for what is right.[25]

Galatians 3:10

But those who depend on the law to make them right with God are under his curse, for the Scriptures say, "Cursed is everyone who does not observe and obey all the commands that are written in God's Book of the Law."[26]

In saying that Jesus bore our sins in His body, Peter is saying that Jesus took the punishment that we deserve for our sins, which is the wrath of God. Paul says in Galatians that Jesus became a curse for us. If these verses are true, then there is no more wrath left for those for whom Christ died. If God would ever pour out any wrath on a Christian, He would be unjust. He would be double-charging because He already charged Jesus.

Hear me, Christian! God is not mad at you. Any and all anger He had against you was poured out upon His Son. His wrath looks like those nine catastrophes mentioned in Revelation. He is not saving some of that for you. He is not going to give you a few of the malignant sores to satisfy His wrath. He is not going to give you a mild version of skin cancer from the scorching sun to pay you back for your sins. He will allow unpleasant experiences in your life, but those are always for your good. Romans 8:28 says:

And we know that God causes everything to work together for the good of those who love God and are called according to his purpose for them.[27]

"All things" means exactly that - all things - even our sin. At first glance, that seems heretical, but it is true nonetheless. The bad things that God allows in a Christian's life are never a result of His vengeance, anger, or wrath. They will be used for good, even if they are the earthly consequences of our own sin. Just think about that for a second. God will use the earthly consequences of our own sin for our own good because He causes all things to work together for us.

The wrath Christians deserve has already been poured out on Jesus. I have been preaching and teaching that God has no anger for Christians for well over two decades. I first wrote about it in a book called No Good Christians. You would not believe the flack I received from the religious. People stuck in dead religion just cannot accept the idea that God is not mad at us anymore.

But that is the gospel. If God is keeping track of everything we do and if He gets mad at us every time we sin, then why did Jesus come? What was the purpose of the death of Jesus? He came to remove the barrier of our behavior from relationship with the Father. The way He removed the barrier was to remove our sins as far as away as the east is from the west. If there are no sins that the Father sees on our account, how can He be mad at us? How can God ever be mad at a Christian? It is not possible. That is extremely good news. Believe that good news. Wake up every morning with the knowledge that God is on your side. He loves you. He is not mad at you. There may be struggles and problems in your life, but He is going to be there with you through those struggles, and He is going to use them for good.

And if you are not a Christian, you have got to get in on this deal. That sounds like I am selling car stereos on television or something, but seriously, think about it. It is the offer of the universe. The Creator of everything that exists, Who is most Holy, has provided a way for you to **never** come under His wrath. What we read earlier about God's wrath sounds terrifying. But you never have to come under that wrath if you accept the payment that Jesus made for you. What is stopping you from getting right with God right now? He has done it all. Just give up and accept the gift. There is no minimum behavioral, moral requirement. If there were, none of us would meet it. So again, just answer His knock on your heart's door. You will never be the same. I guarantee it.

Lie #4 God Gets Disappointed With Christians

Jonathan Merritt, a columnist for Religion News Service, tells the following story:

A friend of mine who was raised in a fundamentalist home told me a disturbing story recently. One Sunday morning, the youth pastor at her Southern Baptist Church passed out three-inch galvanized nails to all the students in his care. He instructed them to keep these in their pockets at all times. Whenever they had an impure thought or disrespected their parents or sinned in any way, he told them to place their hand into their pockets and poke the nail into their finger.
"That way you'll be reminded of the pain your[sic] causing God," he said, "and you'll know how disappointed He is with you in that moment." [28]

I have experienced something similar. I was on the worship team at a church. One Sunday morning, the pastor said from the pulpit:

Here's what God wants to say to you. I love you, but you're a mess.

I believe both of those pastors were teaching false doctrine. Neither of those stories shows the heart of God for His children nor the heart of Jesus for His church.

Have you ever heard this lie in church? People say that Christians should be held to a higher standard of behavior.

John MacArthur, one of the most famous and respected Bible teachers living today, says the following in his book, The Gospel According to Jesus:

As a part of his saving work, God will produce repentance, faith, sanctification, yieldedness, obedience and ultimately glorification. Since he is not dependent on human effort in producing those elements, an experience that lacks any of them cannot be the saving work of God. [29]

Statements like that cause people to doubt their salvation. But some teachers think doubting one's salvation is beneficial. They believe that it helps us stay diligent. But it is not a good thing for a Christian to doubt their salvation. The problem with MacArthur's statements above is that we are horrible fruit inspectors. No one can know of someone else whether they are in the process of sanctification, nor where they are in that process.

Many cult members look very sanctified. That is what trips us up. We see people who reject the Christian faith and yet appear to lead moral lives. And we form a doctrine in our heads that says we suck as Christians and we are hypocrites. I guess we need to behave more like the cult members, and then we will be more acceptable to God. What nonsensical, legalistic BS.

Have you ever believed that God was disappointed with you? I feel that way sometimes. I struggle with that religious drive we all have, which wants our acceptance by God to be based on our performance.

Some Christians see God as a frustrated monarch, unsatisfied with us, wondering if we will ever pull our heads out of our - well - you know the euphemism.

Some people see God as disappointed with all Christians, although often they exempt themselves. They will tell you that if you would just be more like them, get up at 5:00 a.m. every day and pray on your knees on a hard cement floor - even when you are on vacation - you may be a little less of a disappointment to God.

Some Christians like me look at themselves and cannot understand why God is **not** disappointed. I tend to be pretty self-critical. Just ask my wife.

We need to settle this issue once and for all. That is what we will do in this chapter. I will come back to this chapter myself when the devil tries to tell me the lie that God is frowning on me when I sin. Yes, I still sin. So do you. If any of you say you do not, you have just committed the sin of bearing false witness.

Anyone who tells you they no longer sin is a liar. I am sorry for being so harsh, but that is the truth. Why else would Paul have even written Romans 7, where he says he is a *wretched* man? Why else would John say, if we claim to have no sin, we're only fooling ourselves and not living in the truth? So here are the facts.

- God is Holy.
- We are sinful.
- Christ died on the cross to pay for our sins.

- God was satisfied.
- God no longer holds our sin against us.

Romans 10:9-10 states:

If you openly declare that Jesus is Lord and believe in your heart that God raised him from the dead, you will be saved. For it is by believing in your heart that you are made right with God, and it is by openly declaring your faith that you are saved.[30]

Notice that these verses teach us that, by believing, one is made right with God and, by confessing one's faith, they are saved from hell.

Also, notice that it does not say that if you believe in Jesus, you are right with God until you mess up. Right-standing with God comes from believing that Jesus is the Messiah. If you are a Christian, you have right-standing with the Father.

In light of even just these two verses, can God be disappointed with those who have trusted in Jesus for their salvation? That is really the question we are answering. To answer this question, let's look at what disappointment really is. Disappointment has two components: **surprise** and **frustration**. Frustration is defined as feeling discouragement or defeat. Let's see how they would apply if God is disappointed with a Christian.

First, God would have to be surprised that a Christian failed to meet expectations. Next, God would have to feel discouragement and defeat when a Christian fails. That is what it means to be frustrated.

Does that sound like the God you know? If it does, you have a wrong picture of God. I know that is a bold thing to say, but God has been encouraging us at Grace Online Church to be bolder in 2021, so we are just getting started.

Let's take a look at Scripture to see if God is ever surprised. Isaiah 41:21-23 says the following:

"Present the case for your idols," says the Lord. "Let them show what they can do, "says the King of Israel. "Let them try to tell us what happened long ago so that we may consider the evidence. Or let them tell us what the future holds, so we can know what's going to happen. Yes, tell us what will occur in the days ahead. Then we will know you are gods.[31]

And then again in Isaiah. 42:8-9:

"I am the Lord; that is my name! I will not give my glory to anyone else, nor share my praise with carved idols. Everything I prophesied has come true, and now I will prophesy again. I will tell you the future before it happens."[32]

You see, for God to be surprised, He would have to lose His sovereignty. The Bible uses the word sovereign about God two-hundred ninety-one times. I think God is trying to tell us that nothing takes Him by surprise. So there goes one of the components of disappointment. God cannot be surprised.

What about frustration? Is God ever frustrated with Christians? Does God feel discouraged or defeated when a Christian sins? Again, let's look at Scripture.

These next verses I am about to show you are so misinterpreted that they are made to say the exact opposite of what they mean.

Ephesians 1:3-5:

All praise to God, the Father of our Lord Jesus Christ, who has blessed us with every spiritual blessing in the heavenly realms because we are united with Christ. Even before he made the world, God loved us and chose us in Christ to be holy and without fault in his eyes. God decided in advance to adopt us into his own family by bringing us to himself through Jesus Christ. This is what he wanted to do, and it gave him great pleasure.[33]

Verse three above says that God has blessed us with every spiritual blessing in the heavenly realms. Just think about that for a second. He does not say that God has blessed us with every material blessing in the earthly realms. I am not sure what spiritual blessings in heaven are, but I cannot wait to find out.

Why did He bless us with those blessings? Because we lead perfect, sinless lives? No. We received the blessings because we are "*united with Christ*." He has already seen our whole life, and He chose us before we took our first breath.

Then, in verse four, it says that God loved us and chose us in Christ to be holy and without fault in His eyes. This verse is very powerful because of two very important words. Imagine this verse without those two words.

God loved us and chose us to be holy and without fault in his eyes.

That would have put all the burden of holiness and faultlessness on us, but those two words - **in Christ** - changed the entire meaning. We are hidden in Christ, and therefore we are holy and faultless.

I know we are piling up a ton of verses, but that is how much grace permeates the Word of God. So, in that spirit, here is yet another.

Galatians 2:20:

My old self has been crucified with Christ. It is no longer I who live, but Christ lives in me. So I live in this earthly body by trusting in the son of God, who loved me and gave himself for me.[34]

We are hidden in Christ. Our old self was crucified with Him. For God to be disappointed with a Christian, He would have to be looking at our flesh, our old self. But that was crucified. It is no longer alive. That is what the above verse says. Instead, Christ Himself lives in me, and I am hidden in Him.

How could God be disappointed with Christ? It is not possible. However, it is possible for our three enemies to try to convince us that God is disappointed. And what are those three enemies? The Bible teaches that a Christian's three enemies are the world, the flesh, and the devil. As we discussed with Lie #2, all three of them are liars.

I recently lost my day job. Some of the reasons were my own fault (remember, I do not claim to be anything other than an imperfect sinner, saved by grace). I was in a funk for weeks after that. I was disappointed with myself, and the enemy started with his fiery darts. Thoughts kept invading my mind and tormenting me - thoughts like:

"You claim to be a Christian. You even told your co-workers that you're a Christian, and then you fail at your job. You are a hypocrite and a poor example of Jesus."

But God knew before time began that I would lose that job. And God knew that the loss of that job would hurt. God also knew that He had something else He wanted me to do. Now, some of you might think, Rick, are you saying that God used your lack of one hundred percent stellar performance in your job for your good and His glory? Yes! That is exactly what I am saying. It is unfortunate that many Christians would say that I failed to glorify God by being fired.

"After all, you're supposed to do your work as unto the Lord. Rick, you are a bad testimony".

But I was not where God wanted me to be, and I was pretty miserable. But I take the responsibility of providing for my family very seriously. So, I just tried to hang in there, even though I was unhappy. I think God knew that I was not going to leave on my own. So, He worked all things together for my good, even getting fired, because then we were able to start Grace Online Church.

But during the time when I was being hard on myself for getting fired, God was not the least bit disappointed with me. In fact, true to His word, He was causing my firing to be used for His glory. How can I say that? Because the Bible says that God causes all things to work together for good, for those who love Him. "All things" means ALL things, even my firing.

And although God was not disappointed with me, He felt **my** disappointment and, like a good Father, He did not just give me some platitude like "You'll do better next time." Instead, I felt His presence and His empathy in the midst of my self-condemnation. He knows when we are disappointed with ourselves, and His response is always grace, love, mercy, and kindness.

Instead of God wagging His finger at me for failing, I believe He had His arm around me (spiritually, of course), feeling my disappointment and telling me that something better was coming. Listen, Christian, God is not disappointed with you. Ever. He is not disappointed with you because of the cross, because Jesus paid for all of your sins, shortcomings, failures, and mistakes. He paid for all of them before you were born. And He did this for a simple reason. We read it earlier in Ephesians 1:5:

God decided in advance to adopt us into his own family by bringing us to himself through Jesus Christ. This is what he wanted to do, and it gave him great pleasure.[35]

God takes pleasure in removing your sin an infinite distance from your account. Jesus said in Luke 12:32:

So don't be afraid, little flock, for it gives your father great happiness to give you the kingdom.[36]

Jesus is saying that to you right now. Don't be afraid. God loves you, and it makes Him very happy to give you heaven. It makes Him very happy to place the kingdom of God inside of you. Luke 17:21 says that is where the kingdom of God is - inside of us. In Ephesians 2:6, the apostle Paul says:

For he raised us from the dead along with Christ and seated us with him in the heavenly realms because we are united with Christ Jesus.[37]

How can God be disappointed with those who are not only **in** Christ but are seated **with** Christ in heavenly realms? How can He say that we are already seated with Christ? Because He sees the end from the beginning, and His plan is perfect. He is not disappointed with His Son Jesus. Therefore, He is not disappointed with you and never will be - if you are in Jesus.

Now, if you do not have a relationship with Jesus, maybe you feel Him moving on you right now. I remember when it happened to me. I had been in church services for 20 years. But one Sunday, it was like my eyes were opened to the fact that Jesus paid for all of my sins and failures on the cross. I felt a little nervous. What should I do with this new revelation? That was actually proof that God was calling me to salvation that day. So, I prayed a prayer and invited

Jesus into my heart. And I would like to lead you in a similar prayer right now.

If you do not have a real relationship with Jesus, pray with me now.

Heavenly Father. Thank You for sending your Son to die on the cross to pay for my sins. I know that I am a sinner. I know that I need You, God. I feel You knocking at my heart's door. I now open my heart and invite You in. I accept this free gift of forgiveness and salvation. Thank You for loving me so much. In Jesus's name, Amen.

If you prayed that prayer for the first time in your life just now, you just became a Christian. You just received eternal life. God will never leave you. You will have struggles because they are common to all humans. But you will never be alone again. The Holy Spirit will take up residence in your heart, guaranteeing your permanent salvation. Do me a favor. If that describes you, come by and see me in heaven 1,000 years from now. We can share a cup of living water and maybe a cannoli. And yes, of course, there are cannoli in the kingdom of God. Have you ever had one? They are heavenly!

54

Lie #5 The Holy Spirit Convicts Christians Of Sin

Of all of the lies that we cover in this book, debunking this one has changed me the most. I expect this chapter to get the most criticism of any in this book. In light of that, would you please do me a favor? Read to the end of the chapter before you judge its veracity. Some of the criticism we will get regarding this topic will be from Christians who have been taught error. But some will come from the teachers of that error if God allows them to see this message. I sincerely pray that God will allow that, not for my sake but for the sake of the gospel.

Ok, here we go. First, as Trinitarians, we believe that the Holy Spirit is God, right? The idea that God convicts Christians of sin comes from a gross misinterpretation of John 16:7-11.

But in fact, it is best for you that I go away, because if I don't, the Advocate won't come. If I do go away, then I will send him to you. And when he comes, he will convict the world of its sin, and of God's righteousness, and of the coming judgment. The world's sin is that it refuses to believe in me. Righteousness is available because I go to the Father, and you will see me no more. Judgment will come because the ruler of this world has already been judged.[38]

Jesus says here that He will send the Advocate. What on Earth does that mean? I think most Christians understand that Jesus is talking about the Holy Spirit here, but why did He choose the word advocate?

Let's look at the Greek word Jesus uses here, which is *parakletos.* When I typed that into my Mac, it was auto-corrected to *parakeets.* No, Jesus did not promise to send us parakeets, although they are pretty cool. The definition of *parakletos:*

intercessor, consoler, advocate, comforter.

Let's look at each of these synonyms to see if we can get a clearer understanding of who Jesus was going to send and what the *parakletos* would do.

An **intercessor** is someone who prays to the Father for us when we do not know what to pray. Romans 8:26 clearly states this. A **consoler** is one who alleviates grief, a sense of loss, or trouble. An **advocate** is a lawyer who fights for his client. A **comforter** is one who gives strength and hope.

Jesus promised to send us the Holy Spirit, who would pray for us when we do not know what to pray, alleviate our grief, fight for us, and give us strength and hope. Do you get the picture so far? This is who Jesus sent to the church at Pentecost. Then Jesus tells us what the Holy Spirit will do when He comes.

he will convict the world of its sin, and of God's righteousness, and of the coming judgment.

He will convict **the world** of its sin and of God's righteousness and of the coming judgment. I am so glad that Jesus did not stop speaking there, because if He did, maybe - and it's a big maybe - one might think that there is justification to believe that the Holy Spirit convicts Christians of sin. But He goes on. Jesus says:

the world's sin is that it refuses to believe in me.

There are two very important ideas that we need to recognize here.

First, it is the **world** that the Holy Spirit is convicting. This verse says nothing about the Holy Spirit convicting a Christian. And second, the Holy Spirit is convicting the world for one sin only, the sin of unbelief. People will go to hell for not believing in Jesus because they will remain culpable for their sins. That is the clear message of the gospel.

And just to clarify more, the word used for convict in Greek is *elegcho*. The definition of this word is:

To convict, refute, confute, generally with a suggestion of shame to the person convicted

Pay attention to that word - **shame**. Shame is part of the convicting of the Holy Spirit. So, the first question we need to ask is this:

Did Jesus send us an intercessor, consoler, advocate, and comforter to cause Christians to feel shame?

NO!

Does shaming a Christian sound like something God does? We have seriously screwed this up in the evangelical church. Do you know what the opposite of conviction is? It is acquittal or justification. Justification means:

to be shown to be just or right

We need to be just and right to be with the Lord forever. That is a fact. What we believe about how we are justified determines whether we have accepted the true gospel or false gospel. The reformers fought for the concept of *justification by faith*. In their day, the church was so corrupt that it charged people money for justification. These were called *indulgences*. Essentially, if you paid the church a certain amount of money, depending on which sin you were about to commit, then you could go ahead and commit the sin, and God would not hold it against you. Literally, they were teaching that you could pre-purchase forgiveness and justification. But John Calvin, Martin Luther, and others publicly pointed out this corruption, and the Reformation was born. I am afraid that, in the five hundred or so years since the Reformation, Protestantism has slid back and almost become unreformed. It is like the Reformation never happened. Therefore, it is crucial that we understand, or if necessary, rediscover the doctrine of justification by faith.

Another way to say *justification by faith* is:

made right with God by believing.

Does the Bible teach justification by faith? Well, let's take a look. Romans 3:26b states:

God did this to demonstrate his righteousness, for he himself is fair and just, and he makes sinners right in his sight when they believe in Jesus.

That is justification by faith - being made right when we *believe*. But wait, there's more! Romans 10:9-10:

If you openly declare that Jesus is Lord and believe in your heart that God raised him from the dead, you will be saved. For it is by believing in your heart that you are made right with God, and it is by openly declaring your faith that you are saved. [39]

Did you see that in verse ten? It is by believing in your heart that you were **made right with God**. That is justification. What do you have to believe in your heart? Well, the verse answers that question. Believe in your heart that God raised Jesus from the dead. That means to believe that Jesus is who He said He was, the Messiah, the Son of God. Paul says in Romans 1 that the resurrection proves Jesus is God. In verse 4, Paul says.

And he was shown to be the son of God when he was raised from the dead by the power of the Holy Spirit. He is Jesus Christ, our Lord. [40]

Believing in your heart is what makes you right with God. What do you need to believe? You must believe that Jesus was raised from the dead by the Father, which showed Him to be the son of God.

Again, Paul tells us in 1 Corinthians 15:17:

And if Christ has not been raised, then your faith is useless and you are still guilty of your sins.[41]

I want to state the converse of that verse:

*If Christ **has** been raised from the dead, your faith is useful and you are no longer guilty of your sins.*

This next question is of utmost importance. If believing in the resurrection of Jesus makes you right with God, and therefore you are no longer guilty of your sins, how in the world could the Holy Spirit convict you of those sins? How can God (the Holy Spirit) convict someone whom God (the Father) has acquitted? He cannot. It is impossible.

Now, people who teach what I have just taught are often accused of promoting *hyper-grace*. Those who call this hyper-grace say that we are offering a dangerous and unbiblical teaching that leads people down a licentious path to hell. They also say that those who teach this (I guess that means me) will be held accountable for the spiritual death of millions. They say that we must continually confess our sins to God or *"keep short accounts"* with God. But does the word say that?

Well, many say that 1 John 1:9 shows that we must continually confess. Let's see if that is what it says.

But if we confess our sins to him, he is faithful and just to forgive us our sins and cleanse us from all wickedness.[42]

There are a few things we need to understand about 1 John 1:9, concepts that should be a part of all of our Bible study:

context and **audience.**

John was writing to a church in Asia that was struggling with Gnosticism. Gnosticism taught that the flesh was not real, and therefore, sin was not real. According to Gnostics, the flesh and sin are illusions. They even believed that the resurrected Christ was an illusion and that Jesus was not physically resurrected. According to them, it was an apparition.

This heresy had invaded the church, so John addresses it. That is why he says in verse eight:

If we claim to have no sin, we are only fooling ourselves and not living in the truth.[43]

He is telling the Gnostics that they are fooling themselves by believing that the flesh and sin are illusions. He uses the word *we* there in an instructive way. We all use the word *we* that way sometimes. It could sound like this:

"Now, little Joey, we do not throw food in this house, do we?"

Do you see? In other words, John is saying to the Gnostics:

"Hey, you guys are saying we don't sin. But if we say that, we're only fooling ourselves, and the truth isn't in us.

He is trying to get the Gnostics to see that their sinful flesh is not an illusion. It is real, and therefore it will send them to hell if they are not forgiven. But then, He offers the answer to the Gnostics. Instead of agreeing with them that they have no need of forgiveness, he says:

If we confess our sins, God forgives them and cleanses us from all wickedness. [42]

John is preaching the gospel to people who thought they were Christians but were not. They believed they had no sin and that sin was an illusion. He knows that their doctrine of salvation is in error, and therefore, they are lost. Then, John gives them the answer. It is that simple. Read the whole chapter. He focuses on proving that Jesus was actually physically resurrected. John says the Apostles touched the resurrected Christ with their own hands. He is showing that the body is not an illusion. Their flesh is not an illusion. Sin is not an illusion. And they needed to confess that they are sinners.

This is not talking about Christians constantly confessing and then receiving forgiveness each time they sin. That is absurd. Who could do that anyway? Do you remember every sin you have ever committed? I definitely do not. No one could ever remain saved if this were the proper interpretation of these verses, because the Bible also says in James 2:10:

For the person who keeps all of the laws except one is as guilty as a person who has broken all of God's laws. [44]

If the legalistic interpretation of 1 John 1:9 is true - *keep short accounts with God* - then Christians need to continually confess to remain forgiven. And, if you forget to confess just one sin, guess what! According to James 2:10, you are as guilty as Hitler.

I am sorry if that offends you, but it is not hyperbole. If those legalists want to accuse us of hyper-grace, they need to level that same charge against the Apostles Peter, John, James, and even Jesus. Peter said in 1 Peter 1:2:

God the Father knew you and chose you long ago, and his Spirit has made you holy. As a result, you have obeyed him and have been cleansed by the blood of Jesus Christ.

May God give you more and more grace and peace.[45]

Hey, that sounds a little "hyper" there. As a result of God's choosing you, you obeyed the gospel. You believed. Peter goes on to say that grace does not end at salvation. He asks God to give us more and more grace and peace. The Greek here says,

"may God give you an abundance of grace and peace."

That also sounds "hyper." The Apostle John, the same guy that wrote 1 John 1:9 and John 3:16, also wrote John 1:16:

From his abundance we have all received one gracious blessing after another.[46]

That sounds like hyper-blessings.

What did Jesus's brother, James, have to say about this? He says in James 4:6:

And he gives grace generously. As the Scriptures say, "God opposes the proud but gives grace to the humble."[47]

Ok, what about the greatest teacher of all, Jesus Christ? Jesus taught about the prodigal son, who had sinned against his father, wasted everything, and wished his father were dead. And yet, when his father saw him coming back home, he ran to his son. The son started to confess, but the father interrupted his confession and began celebrating. He celebrated because this son was dead to him, but now he was alive. The father did not ask to be paid back. The father did not ask for a heartfelt confession that apologized for every way in which he was wronged. The father accepted his son, welcomed him home, and had a party.

Let's check out another parable of Jesus. This is the parable of the pharisee and the tax collector. It is in Luke 18:9-14:

Then Jesus told this story to some who had great confidence in their own righteousness and scorned everyone else:

Let's stop right there for the moment. Do you remember that I earlier wrote that we have to understand to whom a particular Scripture was addressed? Well, here, Dr. Luke tells us directly who the audience is. He says this is addressed to *legalists*, right? It is addressed to those who had great confidence in their righteousness and scorned everyone else. Wow! That is the definition of legalism. Jesus is telling a story to combat legalism. We must keep this in mind when reading this parable.

"Two men went to the Temple to pray. One was a Pharisee, and the other was a despised tax collector. The Pharisee stood by himself and prayed this prayer: 'I thank you, God, that I am not like other people—cheaters, sinners, adulterers. I'm certainly not like that tax collector! I fast twice a week, and I give you a tenth of my income.'

"But the tax collector stood at a distance and dared not even lift his eyes to heaven as he prayed. Instead, he beat his chest in sorrow, saying, 'O God, be merciful to me, for

I am a sinner.' I tell you, this sinner, not the Pharisee, returned home justified before God. For those who exalt themselves will be humbled, and those who humble themselves will be exalted."[48]

The tax collector just asked for grace and mercy, realizing he had nothing to offer in return.

Now, check out verse 14:

*I tell you the truth, this sinner, not the Pharisee, returned home **justified** before God.*

That sounds like hyper-grace - grace without conditions. The final verse I want to use here to show that hyper-grace is Biblical is Romans 5:20. For this one, just to show that I am not a New Living Translation only proponent, we will use the King James Version.

Moreover, the law entered that the offense might abound, but where sin abounded, grace did much more abound.[49]

Guess which Greek word is translated into *"did much more abound."* It is *huperperisseuo,* and it means *hyper-abounded.* That sounds like hyper-grace to me.

Now, before we go any further, I know some of you are worrying that I believe in an actual heretical doctrine called *hyper-grace.* I want to make a distinction. I believe that grace is as hyper as it can be. It is a well deeper than we could ever drain. But there is a teaching called *hyper-grace* that is antinomian, and we get accused of teaching *antinomianism.* That word means "against law." Antinomians teach that no Biblical commands have any benefit for a Christian because it is all grace. We absolutely do not teach that and stand against it.

What we do teach is that your sin very well may cause you horrible consequences on Earth, even if you are a Christian. But a Christian's sin cannot have the consequence of damnation.

I believe we have shown here that the Holy Spirit does not convict Christians of sin because He is God, and God has removed our sin as far as the east is from the west. How could the Holy Spirit declare guilty those whom God has declared not guilty? He cannot. The Holy Spirit convicts the world, not Christians. Now, you may be thinking,

"What's that feeling I get after I sin? I feel very bad sometimes. Isn't that the conviction of the Holy Spirit?"

No, it is not. It is your spirit, your renewed conscience, reminding you that your flesh is fallen and not redeemable. It feels icky. We love the Lord, so we do not feel good when we sin. But what does the Holy Spirit do in those times? Do you remember the definition of paraclete? He intercedes. He prays to the Father to show us that we are in Christ. He tells the Father, "confirm their faith." He consoles us. He knows we feel bad and that our conscience is condemning us. So, He consoles us. He advocates for us. He says, "Father, remember, this sin is already forgiven," when the devil, the accuser of the brethren, accuses us before God. And He comforts us. He relieves our stress, sadness, and pain.

The Holy Spirit, God, cannot convict someone whom the Father, God, has acquitted. It is that simple.

If you have not yet believed in Jesus, His death for you, and His resurrection, you may be feeling the conviction of the Holy Spirit. Remember, He convicts the world of the sin of unbelief. If you are an unbeliever, I say to you, "Believe! Right now!" This is the day of salvation. Ask Jesus to forgive your sins and come into your heart. He will do it. And He will never convict you because you will have been declared not guilty forever. You will be free, and whom the Son sets free is free indeed.

I want to close this chapter with one last Scripture. Romans 8:33-34:

Who dares accuse us whom God has chosen for his own? No one—for God himself has given us right standing with himself. Who then will condemn us? No one—for Christ Jesus died for us and was raised to life for us, and he is sitting in the place of honor at God's right hand, pleading for us.[50]

The Holy Spirit does not convict Christians of sin. That is a big fat lie from the pit of hell.

68

Lie #6 Repentance Is Your Part In Salvation Equation

If you thought the last chapter was controversial, buckle up. This chapter may get some pushback. Again, I ask you to read the whole chapter with an open mind before deciding that I am a heretic.

We hear a lot about repentance in Christian circles. It seems to be a big part of the salvation deal. In fact, it is essential to salvation.

If it is that important, we should understand what it is and what it has to do with us. In this chapter, we will answer three questions:

- What is repentance?
- Is repentance necessary?
- From where does repentance come?

So, let's start with the first question.

Question 1: What is repentance?

The word used for repentance in Greek is *metanoia*. It literally means:

to think better or to change one's mind for the better

The first part of the word - *meta* - means:

beyond, after, better, above.

I am sure you studied metamorphosis in elementary school. That is when a caterpillar changes into a butterfly. The *morph* in metamorphosis means *change,* and the *meta* means *to a better state.*

So, we have thoroughly defined *meta.* Now, what does the *noia* part of metanoia mean? *Noia* means *thought.* So, repent literally means to think better - to change your mind. Repentance is not:

- feeling sorry.
- changing your behavior.
- confessing every one of your sins to God.
- promising that you will do better or even never do a certain sin again.

Repentance means a change of mind. Another way of thinking about repentance is *to wake up - to come to your senses.*

Now, let's look at Scripture. In Mark 1, we see repentance used in a few ways. First, we see in verse 4:

John the Baptist appeared in the wilderness preaching a baptism of repentance for the forgiveness of sin.[51]

John the Baptist preached the message of human commitment. Change your mind as an act of your will. Turn to God and be baptized. He was preparing the way for the gospel. He was not preaching the gospel of the kingdom.

He was preaching, "Repent! Prepare the way because God is coming."

Have you ever seen those shirts or memes that say something like, "Jesus is coming, and boy is he pissed" or "Jesus is coming. Look busy?" These are funny, and I am sure they probably offend some, but that is similar to what John the Baptist was preaching. My paraphrase of his message is:

"Prepare the way of the Lord. The Lord is coming. Change your mind about God and get ready and be baptized to memorialize and commemorate this changing of your mind."

Now then, in the same chapter, Jesus gets baptized by John and begins His ministry. Jesus immediately goes into the wilderness for forty days. He was tempted by the devil there.

When He comes back, Jesus begins preaching. This time He is preaching the gospel of the kingdom, the gospel of God. Check out Mark 1:14-15. We'll use the KJV for this verse:

Now after that John was put in prison, Jesus came into Galilee, preaching the gospel of the kingdom of God, and saying, "The time is fulfilled, and the kingdom of God is at hand: repent ye, and believe the gospel."[52]

Here, **repent** and **believe the gospel** are saying the same thing. Change your mind so that now you believe the good news that I am proclaiming. Accept it. Agree with it.

What is repentance? It is to change one's mind, to think better. That is all it means. In order to understand its meaning in the multitude of verses in which it is used, context and audience must be taken into account. We have made a theological concept out of the Greek word *metanoia*, and some have attempted to dive deeply into this concept as if it is a stand-alone act that shows one is serious with God. Then, they superimpose that meaning every time they see the word *repent* in the Bible. Repentance (*metanoia*) can be used in a variety of ways. I could order chocolate ice cream and then repent and order vanilla. There is nothing spiritual there. Metanoia can be used in many ways because we can change our minds about many things. Repentance is simply a change of mind about something. What that something is depends on the context in which repentance is used.

Question 2: Is repentance necessary for salvation?

Is a change of mind necessary for salvation? We already saw in Mark 1:15, Jesus said, "repent and believe in the gospel." Let's see what happens when we substitute *change your mind* for *repent*.

change your mind and believe in the gospel

Changing your mind from unbelief is the same thing as believing. Whenever we see repent and believe in the same verse, they are synonyms. It is the same as saying, "Stop not believing and start believing."

Is repentance necessary for salvation? Absolutely. You must have a change of mind about the gospel. If you are a rejector of the gospel, you have to become an acceptor of the gospel.

Did you know that the Gospel of John never uses the word repent - *metanoia*? Never. If repentance is something in addition to believing in order to be saved, then something is wrong here. John says the purpose of his book is to preach the gospel. John 20:31 states:

But these are written so that you may continue to believe that Jesus is the Messiah, the Son of God, and that by believing in him you will have life by the power of his name.[53]

The purpose of all John wrote was that we might believe, and by believing, we would be saved. But he never used the word repent. Why not? Because believing in something new means changing one's mind, which is repentance. He did not need the word because he used its synonym - *believe.*

Check out 1 Peter 1:2:

God the Father knew you and chose you long ago, and his Spirit has made you holy. As a result, you have obeyed him and have been cleansed by the blood of Jesus Christ.[54]

This verse says that God chose you and set you apart (that is what *holy* means) before you were born. The next three words are *critically* important - **As a result**. As a result of God choosing you and making you holy, you have obeyed Him and been cleansed by the blood of Jesus. Here, the obedience talked about is obedience to the gospel. Legalists want to make it something else, but it is not.

We saw in the last chapter that believing could not mean obeying the law, ordinances, and commandments because the Bible says if you obey all of that except a single tiny part, it is the same as breaking every law. God is saying to obey the gospel. He is not saying that we need to obey every word that Jesus preached and every word in the Bible in order to be saved. That is not the gospel to obey. It is the opposite of the good news. It is very bad news. The way legalists would have it, we would not be saved if we ever disobeyed anything God has ever said. Some try to qualify this bad theology. I'll bet you have heard of mortal sins and venial sins. None of that matters in God's salvation equation. All sin is sin, and it all disqualifies. If God is saying to obey everything in order to be saved, that would mean salvation is of works. Instead, obey here means obeying the gospel. And what is the gospel? It is this.

Jesus shed his blood to pay for your sins. He wants to enter your spirit and live inside of you, to guide and comfort you. If you open the door by believing (obeying the gospel), God will come into your heart. Change your thinking about Him. You thought He was a charlatan. You thought He was a myth. Change your thinking. Believe. Repent.

Do you get the picture?

The second question was pretty easy to answer. Is repentance necessary? Yes, it is. Now, we move on to the third question.

Question 3: From where does repentance come?

If repentance for salvation simply means to change your mind and believe the gospel, that makes it much easier for us. Right? It is easy to believe, especially if I do not have to confess every sin I have ever committed and repent of each one. Right? No. It is not easy to believe. In fact, it is not possible for us to repent in and of ourselves. It is not possible for us to change our own minds about the gospel. Your natural mind cannot be changed in this way. The Bible says this in 1 Corinthians 2:14:

But people who aren't spiritual can't receive these truths from God's Spirit. It all sounds foolish to them and they can't understand it, for only those who are spiritual can understand what the Spirit means.[55]

We need a new heart, a renewed mind. That comes at regeneration, and then we repent. I know that sounds weird, but it is true. Our natural mind cannot understand the things of God. Your natural mind cannot change its own opinion of the gospel. This was clearly taught by the Reformers.

The gospel will always be foolishness to the natural man. So that must mean something other than the natural man needs to accept the gospel. We need to be regenerated first. Now, that cannot be right, can it? Is God the first Actor, even in repentance? Well, again, let's let Scripture answer that question. 2 Timothy 2:24-26 says:

A servant of the Lord must not quarrel but must be kind to everyone, be able to teach, and be patient with difficult people. Gently instruct those who oppose the truth. Perhaps God will change those people's hearts, and they will learn the truth. Then they will come to their senses and escape from the devil's trap. For they have been held captive by him to do whatever he wants.[56]

Do you see that? God has to change a person's heart before they come to their senses - before they repent. Let's look at Acts 11:18:

When the others heard this, they stopped objecting and began praising God. They said, "We can see that God has also given the Gentiles the privilege of repenting of their sins and receiving eternal life."[57]

Here is an analogy. If you were God and you told a group of humans to fly, they may say, "But we can't. We don't have wings." But if you then supernaturally gave those people wings, you could tell them to fly, and they could do it.

Did you ever notice that militant atheists say that religion is a tool for control? They are absolutely correct. Legalistic religion binds us to a system of rules so that we can be less of a problem to church leaders and to God. Legalists will hound you to repent and keep repenting. They will find everything that you are doing wrong - or that they *think* is wrong - and they will tell you to repent of that.

For example, we sometimes hint at curse words in our sermons and posts. We *call BS* sometimes. You would not believe how many Christians get uptight about that; talk about straining at gnats and swallowing camels. In their view of what the Christian life should be, there is no place for the initials BS. So, they literally dismiss everything our ministry teaches. What a shame that is. Legalism robs them of the chance to hear messages that would make them much freer.

I guess it is risky for a pastor to say to a church,

"You don't need me to hound you about your behavior. God lives in you. He will guide you."

You may have a church where people let their sin show a little more, but at least you would have a more honest church. Really, repentance means just that. Repentance means being honest with God and rethinking how you relate to Him because of the gospel of grace.

I have one more Scripture. Paul and Barnabas are preaching the gospel in Antioch to a crowd of people in Acts 13:48:

When the Gentiles heard this, they were very glad and thanked the Lord for his message; and all who were chosen for eternal life became believers.[58]

The ability to believe does not come from you. You need a new heart. Those in the crowd, who were chosen and had already been given a new heart, believed. They changed their thinking. They repented.

Repentance is not **your** part in the salvation equation. Repenting means changing your mind about the gospel. You cannot do that until you have a new mind, a new heart. The good news is that God miraculously gives you this as a gift. Ezekiel 36:26 says:

And I will give you a new heart, and I will put a new spirit in you. I will take out your stony, stubborn heart and give you a tender, responsive heart.[59]

If this message has resonated with you, maybe you have already been given a new heart. So, again, I have something to say to you. Believe! Repent! Change your thinking! You can do it, but only with your new heart - your new mind. If God is moving on you, maybe pray something like this:

Lord, I now understand that I am not holy, but You are. I think differently about You now, which means You have already given me a new heart. So, from that new heart, I repent of the sin of unbelief. I now believe that You died for me and rose from the dead. And I ask You to come into my life.

He will do it, and all of your sins will be forgiven. As many of you as are pointed to eternal life when you are reading these words will believe. There is no need to continually show God how sorry you are. He may use sorrow in your life, but your sins are forgiven. And you did not seek God for that forgiveness. Instead, He chose you before the foundation of the world. It takes one thing to be saved. Faith, believing, changing your mind, and repenting are all the same thing. They are all different ways of stating the same single requirement for salvation. And even that one requirement is a gift from God and not as a result of your diligent effort. If you don't believe that, look again at Ephesians 2:8-9:

God saved you by his grace when you believed. And you can't take credit for this; it is a gift from God. Salvation is not a reward for the good things we have done, so none of us can boast about it.[60]

Repenting equals believing. You cannot do it without a new heart. Repenting is not something you continually do as a Christian in order to be forgiven. That is the law. That is religion, and religion **is** a tool to control the masses.

Lie #7 A Loving God Would Never Punish People For Eternity

It used to be that the people who denied the existence of hell were outside of the church. In fact, the reason many rejected the church was that it preached hellfire and brimstone. Their thinking was,

"Those Christians say Jesus loves everyone, but then He sends His children to hell. No way. I can't believe that."

Unfortunately, this insidious lie has invaded the evangelical church. I have several Christian friends who no longer believe in eternal torment. This error comes from false beliefs about both people and God.

The first false belief is that people are basically good. I come from an east coast Italian family. Back east, you often hear the phrase "good person."

It sounds like this.

"Oh, you mean Joey? Oh, he's a good person. Oh, you mean little Frankie at the deli? Yeah, he's a good person."

But does the Bible say that people are basically good? Well, let's take a look at a few verses. Romans 3:9-20 states:

Well then, should we conclude that we Jews are better than others? No, not at all, for we have already shown that all people, whether Jews or Gentiles, are under the power of sin. As the Scriptures say,

"No one is righteous—not even one. No one is truly wise; no one is seeking God. All have turned away; all have become useless. No one does good, not a single one.

Their talk is foul, like the stench from an open grave. Their tongues are filled with lies. Snake venom drips from their lips. Their mouths are full of cursing and bitterness.

They rush to commit murder. Destruction and misery always follow them. They don't know where to find peace.

They have no fear of God at all."

Obviously, the law applies to those to whom it was given, for its purpose is to keep people from having excuses, and to show that the entire world is guilty before God. For no one can ever be made right with God by doing what the law commands. The law simply shows us how sinful we are.[61]

Now, I know those are a lot of verses, but they are remarkable. Paul is saying that no one is good, naturally. In fact, before we are regenerated, we stink. Our talk is a foul stench to God.

We have to understand this. If we do not, we will never understand eternal punishment. We have to understand that no one is good. One of our podcasts is called "No Good Christians." Even Christians are not good in their human nature. Check out this verse that we used to name our podcast. It is Luke 18:18-19:

Once a religious leader asked Jesus this question: "Good Teacher, what should I do to inherit eternal life?"

"Why do you call me good?" Jesus asked him. "Only God is truly good."

Now, you might say, "Come on, no one is as good as God. I get that. But that does not mean we cannot still be a little good, right?"

Well, I have an analogy that might help.

Picture this. I am standing on the beach in California. Let's say it is Huntington Beach. Standing next to me is Michael Phelps. By the way, he has twenty-eight Olympic swimming medals, six of which are gold. We are there for a race. We are going to swim to Hawaii. Someone shoots off a starter pistol, and we are off. After about five minutes, I am done. I have a stitch in my side, and I am coughing up a lung. I swam 50 yards, but Michael is still going. He swims for a half hour and gets two miles out from the shore.

The difference in our swimming prowess is obvious for all to see, as long as you are standing on the shore of Huntington Beach. But if you are standing at the finish line, which is the shore of Hawaii, Michael and I are about the same. Neither of us is close, and you cannot see either of us from Hawaii. In the same way, the Bible teaches that, from God's perspective, no one is good.

We may do some comparing this side of heaven. We have people like Mother Teresa on one end and Hitler on the other. But even Mother Teresa's natural goodness was not impressive to God. Her goodness in helping so many was God working through her. Even she would have told you that.

To settle this issue, the Bible says this in Isaiah 64:6:

We are all infected and impure with sin. When we display our righteous deeds, they are nothing but filthy rags.[62]

Now, I do not want to unnecessarily offend anyone, so I will state the following very delicately. The word *filthy* here in the original Hebrew is *ed,* and it refers to something that happens to women of childbearing age once a month. So, there is that word and then the word rag. Do you get the picture? My good deeds are filthy rags. My swimming and even Michael Phelps swimming are so inferior to the swimming that someone would need to get to Hawaii that, for this task, our abilities do not matter. It does not matter that he is better than me. He is not good enough to swim to Hawaii.

In the same way, it does not matter (from a salvation perspective) if some people seem better to us than others. They are. Mother Teresa did many more good deeds in her life than I probably ever will. But even she fell way short of the requirement, which is perfect holiness. All of us fall way too short. That is the very reason Jesus had to come. We could not make it. We could not stand before a Holy God with that level of human goodness because it is not good - not as God counts goodness. That is the first misunderstanding.

Now let's look at the misunderstanding of God's character, which makes people deny the existence of hell.

1 John 4:8 says that God is love. Let's be clear. Since God is love, He gets to tell us what love is. I wrote a book about

this topic, called "Love Is the Answer." If you want to learn more about the Bible's definition of love, that book may help you.

The misunderstanding about God that contributes to the denial of hell is that people believe that God is **only** love. But that is not all He is. He is also Holy.

But before we get to that, let's take it one level higher. I am sure you would agree with the following statement because it is pretty logical:

If there is a God who deserves to be called God, meaning He is actually omniscient, omnipresent, and omnipotent, He is who He is. What you and I think about Him does not change who He is. We may think He's unfair. That doesn't matter. We may think that He's mean. That doesn't matter either. What matters is that He is God, and He has revealed himself to us in Scripture and also in person. Scripture tells us who God is and what love looks like. And Jesus showed us that love in person.

If you agree that what you and I believe about God does not change Who He is, then we can go to the Bible to learn about God's character. We have already seen in 1 John 4:8 that God is love. If that is the only information we ever had about God, we might conclude that there could not be a hell. But let's look at what else the Bible says about Him.

1 John 1:5 says this:

This is the message we heard from Jesus and now declare to you: God is light, and there is no darkness in him at all.[63]

Darkness cannot be in the presence of God.

Let's look at Acts 5:1-11:

But there was a certain man named Ananias who, with his wife, Sapphira, sold some property. He brought part of the money to the apostles, claiming it was the full amount. With his wife's consent, he kept the rest.

Then Peter said, "Ananias, why have you let Satan fill your heart? You lied to the Holy Spirit, and you kept some of the money for yourself. The property was yours to sell or not sell, as you wished. And after selling it, the money was also yours to give away. How could you do a thing like this? You weren't lying to us but to God!"

As soon as Ananias heard these words, he fell to the floor and died. Everyone who heard about it was terrified. Then some young men got up, wrapped him in a sheet, and took him out and buried him.

About three hours later his wife came in, not knowing what had happened. Peter asked her, "Was this the price you and your husband received for your land?"

"Yes," she replied, "that was the price."

And Peter said, "How could the two of you even think of conspiring to test the Spirit of the Lord like this? The young men who buried your husband are just outside the door, and they will carry you out, too."

Instantly, she fell to the floor and died. When the young men came in and saw that she was dead, they carried her out and buried her beside her husband. Great fear gripped the entire church and everyone else who heard what had happened.[64]

After reading about Ananias and Sapphira, do you still think God is a God of love? I do. But He is also the God of truth and justice. Now, I do not believe God will strike down a Christian for lying. I do not believe that Ananias and Sapphira were truly born again. But we must understand that God is Holy. If He looks upon you without the clothing of Christ's righteousness, you are offensive and cut off from Him. Check out Isaiah 59:2:

It's your sins that have cut you off from God.[65]

In God, there is no darkness, but there is darkness in us. Therefore, if we want to be *in Christ*, then something needs to be done. I hope you are beginning to see the picture that God is not only love. God is also just. He is also the Way, the Truth, and the Life.

Once we have the proper understanding of humans - all are fallen and sinful, and God, Who is not just loving, but also just - we have removed the two main fallacies that cause people to dismiss the concept of hell without even researching it.

And why do we want to dismiss hell in the first place? We do that because it makes us feel better. It sits well with us that everyone should go to heaven except maybe Adolf Hitler and Charles Manson.

But the fact that we would be OK with that shows we are fallen, sinful people because we ignore God's holiness. We treat Him like a nice grandpa who just hugs His kids and does not say much. But that is not how it is. Sin must be punished.

We have shown that it is not outside of God's character for there to be a hell. But does the Bible teach that there is **eternal** punishment?

Let's see what Jesus has to say about hell. In Matthew 25:46, Jesus says:

"And they will go away into eternal punishment, but the righteous will go into eternal life."[66]

Jesus has just told the parable of the sheep and the goats. He says here that the goats will go into **eternal** punishment. I did not invent the concept of "*eternal punishment.*" Jesus taught it.

Notice that there is a balance, a comparison between eternal punishment and eternal life. The punishment is eternal, just like the life is eternal. If the punishment is not really eternal, then maybe redemption is not either. But that is absurd. So, Jesus means exactly what He said. There is eternal punishment.

Let's look at another verse. In Matthew 10:28, Jesus tells us:

"Don't be afraid of those who want to kill your body; they cannot touch your soul. Fear only God, who can destroy both soul and body in hell.[67]

People cannot touch your soul. Fear only God Who can destroy both soul and body in hell. These are Jesus's words. Jesus is affirming that there is a hell. But there is more. Check out Mark 9:47-48:

And if your eye causes you to sin, gouge it out. It's better to enter the Kingdom of God with only one eye than to have two eyes and be thrown into hell, 'where the maggots never die and the fire never goes out.'[68]

Man, that sounds horrible. I want nothing to do with it. I praise God that I am not going to be there, but I am not going to deny hell exists. Here is another verse. In Revelation 14:9-11, an angel is speaking:

Then a third angel followed them, shouting, "Anyone who worships the beast and his statue or who accepts his mark on the forehead or on the hand must drink the wine of God's anger. It has been poured full strength into God's cup of wrath. And they will be tormented with fire and burning sulfur in the presence of the holy angels and the Lamb. The smoke of their torment will rise forever and ever, and they will have no relief day or night, for they have worshiped the beast and his statue and have accepted the mark of his name."[69]

To say that the concept of eternal punishment is not in the Bible, you would have to take out your black Bible highlighter and use it on these verses we have just looked at, plus literally hundreds more. The concept of eternal punishment is all over the Bible. Now, I know the topic of hell is unpleasant, but there is something even more unpleasant. Hear me out on this.

If everyone eventually goes to heaven, here are some necessary implications. An ISIS terrorist who beheads a Christian would end up in heaven right next to that Christian, even if he never repented and believed the gospel. That is a horrific concept. But there is one that is even worse. If everyone goes to heaven, why are we even here on Earth? Why would God not have taken us all home to heaven immediately after we believed? What would be the point of all this suffering and pain we go through? God would just be sadistic, making us go through all of the nasty stuff that we deal with here on Earth if everyone goes to heaven anyway. Certainly, He could teach us better if we were in heaven and no longer had to deal with this flesh. Why are we still here?

The reason is that God is directing something like a cosmic play. And in this play, He will glorify Himself by demonstrating His amazing attributes. So, He shows love to His chosen, His elect, and He will demand justice for those that remain in their sin. The Bible calls these people *children of the devil* or *vessels created for destruction*. This may not seem fair to us humans. It just feels better to us if no one goes to hell. And it especially does not seem fair if some people are not chosen and therefore are destined for hell. That is just not fair.

But you see, God is not obligated to do what we think is fair. Paul addresses this in Romans 9:18-21:

So you see, God chooses to show mercy to some, and he chooses to harden the hearts of others so they refuse to listen.

Well then, you might say, "Why does God blame people for not responding? Haven't they simply done what he makes them do?"

No, don't say that. Who are you, a mere human being, to argue with God? Should the thing that was created say to

the one who created it, "Why have you made me like this?"
When a potter makes jars out of clay, doesn't he have a
right to use the same lump of clay to make one jar for
decoration and another to throw garbage into?[70]

The idea that a loving God would not punish people for
eternity is a stinking lie. We have so many examples in
Scripture that prove that this lie just does not fly. But there
is good news for Christians and non-Christians alike.

First, here is the good news for Christians. Your past,
present, and future sins are forgiven. There is no possible
way for you to go to hell. Praise God for that!

If you are not a Christian, you may feel a bit scared by what
I have said in this chapter. That is good, actually, because
it shows that God is working in your heart.

If that is you, now is the time for salvation. We have read
Romans 10:9-10 several times so far. Let's read it again:

If you openly declare that Jesus is Lord and believe in your
heart that God raised him from the dead, you will be saved.
For it is by believing in your heart that you are made right
with God, and it is by openly declaring your faith that you
are saved.[39]

So, do that! Believe in your heart that Jesus is the Son of
God, Who died for your sins and was resurrected, proving
that He was God. Confess with your mouth. Tell someone
that you have become a Christian. Tell someone that you
believe in Jesus and have accepted His gift. If you do this,

you will never have to worry about going to hell. You will have eternal life, not eternal punishment.

The remarkable thing is not that God sends people to hell. The remarkable thing is that any of us would be in heaven. We all deserve that eternal punishment. But, praise God, He has made away for us. That way is through receiving a gift. If you have received that gift, never worry about going to hell. If you have not yet received the gift, what are you waiting for?

Lie #8 You Have To Be Willing To Give Up Everything For Jesus In Order To Be Saved

This theological error is taught by maybe the most famous teacher of the Bible out there. I call him the Protestant Pope. This teacher is John MacArthur, and he says the following in "The Gospel According to Jesus":

Those who are not willing to turn from sin, possessions, false religion, or selfishness will find they cannot turn to Christ in faith. [29]

John MacArthur has been preaching what he calls *Lordship Salvation* for years, and he has gotten flack for it in the past. But the flack has died down, and I do not believe it is because he has backed away from this false doctrine. In fact, I believe the controversy has died down because the evangelical church, for the most part, loves this heresy. It feeds our pride.

MacArthur gets this idea of Lordship Salvation from the story of the rich young ruler. Let's look at that passage. Mark 10:17-22 says:

As Jesus was starting out on his way to Jerusalem, a man came running up to him, knelt down, and asked, "Good Teacher, what must I do to inherit eternal life?"

"Why do you call me good?" Jesus asked. "Only God is truly good. But to answer your question, you know the commandments: 'You must not murder. You must not commit adultery. You must not steal. You must not testify

falsely. You must not cheat anyone. Honor your father and mother.'"

"Teacher," the man replied, "I've obeyed all these commandments since I was young."

Looking at the man, Jesus felt genuine love for him. "There is still one thing you haven't done," he told him. "Go and sell all your possessions and give the money to the poor, and you will have treasure in heaven. Then come, follow me."

At this the man's face fell, and he went away sad, for he had many possessions.[71]

As I stated above, based on this passage, MacArthur says the following:

Those who are not willing to turn from sin, possessions, false religion or selfishness will find they cannot turn to Christ and faith.[29]

But is that really what these verses are saying? If not, has MacArthur created an entire ministry on a misinterpretation of Mark 10? Let's dive into these verses.

Look at how the man approached Jesus - running and kneeling. This shows urgency and respect. He asked Jesus a question, "What must I do to inherit eternal life?" Well, first, as evangelicals and as people who value the Reformation, we should already know that there is nothing we can do to inherit eternal life. Even the question is confused. If you do something to get something, it is not an inheritance.

Inheriting means someone gave something to you. So, the man is coming sincerely, but he is asking the wrong question. Jesus refocuses the conversation. The first thing Jesus tells him is, "no one is good but God." That should give us a clue as to the perspective from which Jesus is coming. The man is not good enough, even though he thinks he is. You are not good enough. No one is good enough. And by the way, that is not how inheritances work. So, Jesus is beginning to teach this man a lesson.

The lesson is that this man is not good enough. That is the point of this passage. Jesus's answer is astounding to me. He gives this man the law. Do you believe Jesus was really recommending that this man obey the Ten Commandments in order to go to heaven? Is that the gospel? Of course, it is not. Was Jesus answering this man's question directly, or was He trying to teach this man something and, by doing so, also teach us something? That is what I think Jesus is doing.

In verse 20, the man says that he has kept the Ten Commandments. But, had he? Could this man have kept the Ten Commandments? Can you? Can anyone? No, of course not. So, Jesus knew that this man incorrectly thought he was good. That is why He prefaces the whole conversation in verse 18 with "only God is good." You see, before the conversation develops, Jesus already knows this man's heart, and He is setting up this conversation accordingly. Now let's look at verse 21. After the man says he has obeyed all of the commandments since he was young, the gospel writer Mark says something amazing.

Looking at the man, Jesus felt genuine love for him.

The Greek word for genuine love here is *agapao*. In my book, "Love Is The Answer," I show that *agapao* is the verb form of agape, which is the unconditional love of God. So, if agape is unconditional, does it make sense that Jesus would put behavioral conditions on heaven for this man, whom He genuinely loves? Jesus answered this man's genuine, heartfelt question, "what must I do to go to heaven?" with, **"obey the law, obey the commandments."**

Is that the gospel we preach? Is that the good news? Romans 3:20 says:

For no one can ever be made right with God by doing what the law commands. The law simply shows us how sinful we are.[72]

So, if the law cannot make this guy right, what is Jesus doing here? Jesus is doing exactly what Romans 3:20 says: He is using the law to show this man how sinful he is.

Jesus knew this man before he even got there, so He set him up. His answers were to show that there is not anything we are capable of doing that can get us to heaven. Jesus knew that the guy was not telling the truth when he said he had kept all of the commandments since his youth. So, to prove that the guy is not telling the truth, Jesus gives him something that is much easier to do than keeping all the commandments. Sell everything.

Now, is that easier? Yes. Selling everything is easier than keeping all of the law. Remember, the law is not just the ten commandments. There are 7404 ordinances in the

Bible. This man cannot do the easier thing. Yet, he is claiming he has done the harder thing.

If he had actually kept all the commandments since he was young, he would have easily said,

"Sure. I'll give everything away. No problem. That's nothing compared to never thinking a lustful thought or never hating anyone."

Jesus had before stated that thinking lustful thoughts is the same as adultery, and thinking hateful thoughts is the same as murder. That is what keeping the law means to Jesus, but obviously, this man had a much lower assessment of what keeping the law meant. He would not give up his possessions, which showed the man that he was not as good as he thought he was.

Is Jesus really giving this guy an answer he can follow? No. He is trying to teach the man that there is nothing he can do. Jesus's hidden answer is that the man is asking the wrong question. The question is wrong because of the word "do."

Jesus says if you want to do it, you had better do it perfectly. Put yourself in Jesus's shoes. He knows He is going to die for the sins of this man. He wants to send this man away for now with a teaching that prepares him to receive the gospel after Jesus has resurrected. He loves this man. I am sure that the Lord was kind of laughing inside when He heard this guy assert that he had kept the whole law.

I have shown that the proper understanding of this verse is not that Jesus is preaching the way to get to heaven, but instead showing that there is nothing we can do to get ourselves there. That is the point of this passage. If this passage were teaching that willingness to give up all of your possessions is a prerequisite to salvation, then Jesus answered this question incorrectly, or at least incompletely, every other time it was asked.

Here is a list of verses where Jesus answers this question differently. And in none of these verses does Jesus say we must sell everything, or even that we must look at every area of our life. He simply says, "Believe!" in most of them.

- Mark 16:15-16 - believe and be baptized
- Luke 13:3 - repent
- John 3:16 - believe
- John 3:3 - be born again
- John 3:5 - be born of water and the spirit
- John 3:36 - believe in the Son
- John 5:24 - hear Jesus's words and believe in the Father
- John 6:28-29 - believe

Is Jesus not giving the full gospel before this, and now He corrects Himself with the rich young ruler?

Absolutely not. Earlier in this book, I talked about an indispensable hermeneutic principle. Do not let one verse contradict a multitude of other verses. If it does, your interpretation of that one verse is wrong. That is what happened here with MacArthur.

There is another passage where Jesus does something similar to what He did with this rich young ruler. That is in Luke 10:25-28:

One day an expert in religious law stood up to test Jesus by asking him this question: "Teacher, what should I do to inherit eternal life?"

Jesus replied, "What does the law of Moses say? How do you read it?"

The man answered, "'You must love the Lord your God with all your heart, all your soul, all your strength, and all your mind.' And, 'Love your neighbor as yourself.'"

"Right!" Jesus told him. "Do this and you will live!"[73]

Just do that, and you will live. Can you do that without the indwelling of the Holy Spirit? You know the answer.

So, here in Luke, Jesus is doing the same thing that He did in Mark 10. He is telling this person to do something that is out of his ability to do. The purpose is that, in the end, the person will come to the end of themselves.

Here is yet another example in Scripture. Do you remember the story of the prodigal son? This is Jesus telling a story about how the Father feels when we turn toward Him. Remember, the son wanted to do what McArthur's trying to get us all to do. He wanted to go through each and every thing he had done wrong. He even rehearsed his apology, remember? But his father stopped him when he started giving that apology and said,

"bring the fatted calf because this son was dead and now he's alive."

When the heart turns, it is all over. Nothing more is required. It is God that turns the heart. Promises and commitments are not required.

Salvation truly is *of God*. He truly is the Author and Finisher of our faith. It all starts and ends with His work.

This issue comes down to whether one believes in synergism or monergism with regard to salvation. The reformers fought for the concept of monergism. Let me explain. **Synergism** says that salvation is a cooperative work between two entities, God and the sinner. The sinner does his part, and then God does His part. **Monergism** says that God is the only Actor in salvation. Do you remember that I described the covenant ceremony between God and Abraham in chapter 1? God went through the ceremony by Himself. Abraham made no commitment. That is monergism.

Anyone who looks at the parable of the rich young ruler and comes away with the lesson that says, "Well, some people just aren't willing to count the cost," has missed the entire point of the parable. The whole point of the parable is that no one can pay the cost except Jesus.

I know I have picked on John MacArthur in this chapter, and I am not going to back away from that. I am not attacking him personally. It is **his** doctrine, and he has to be responsible for what he teaches. Am I saying he is not a Christian? No. Am I saying he is not scholarly or knowledgeable? No. What I am saying is that he derived a false doctrine called Lordship Salvation from Scriptures that teach no such thing.

MacArthur says that pastors like me are going to pay severely for preaching the "non-lordship" gospel. Now, our gospel is definitely different than his, so at least one of us is preaching a false gospel. I believe I have shown that the Lordship Salvation gospel is not Biblical. And MacArthur is not the only one preaching it. In fact, it is the default gospel in many, if not most evangelical churches.

Why do we do this? Why do we believe and teach such things? We do this because of the original sin - pride. We want to feel that we are better than other people. We want to be superior. We want to show that we have rightly divided the word. We want to show that we are really committed to God. We want to show that we did our part in salvation. Lordship Salvation tantalizingly appeals to that pride. But the gospel starts and ends with God moving on us. He regenerates us. As a result, our eyes are open to the truth, and we agree with God about our sin after we are regenerated.

Let's look at the story of Lazarus again.

Lazarus was dead in the tomb. He could not answer the Lord because he was dead. Dead people cannot hear. So, the Lord first quickened him, gave him new life, brought him back from the dead, and then the Lord gave a command. "Lazarus, come forth!" And Lazarus obeyed. Lordship Salvation would have had some sort of meeting between Jesus and Lazarus in the spirit, where Jesus gives Lazarus the conditions and his part in the resurrection process. And then Lazarus agrees. And then and only then would Jesus raise him up from the dead.

That is absurd. And it is just as absurd to believe that unregenerate people can make a commitment to God. Now, it is funny that MacArthur agrees that God has to regenerate someone before they can make their commitments to God. And he says that all who are regenerated will do so. So, I always come back to this one question for MacArthur and the others who teach this.

What in the world are you trying to accomplish? Why focus on what we perceive to be someone's level of commitment to Christ as proof of their salvation? If they cannot make that commitment until God regenerates, just preach the pure, foolish gospel of grace and let God worry about who is regenerated and who is not. Do you remember the parable of the wheat and the tares? It is like these people are going around pointing out the tares. Tares are weeds. They grow right next to the wheat. Jesus said to leave them alone until the harvest. Otherwise, you might uproot some of the real wheat. And that is exactly what is happening. That is what these teachers are doing. They are upsetting the real wheat because they believe they have a mission from God to expose all possible tares. But Jesus said to leave the tares alone.

Christian, you know the gospel. You know it was a gift. And you know that you really **do** want God to be Lord over every area of your life. But I will also bet that ninety-nine-point nine percent of you did not go through every possible cost that could be attached to this new life and state your willingness to pay it. That is not how we get saved. God touches our hearts, and we find ourselves able to believe and receive Jesus. That is it. Do not receive this legalistic Lordship BS. And yes, that is what it is. BS.

Adding to the gospel is not a good thing to do. The gospel is simple. You do not have to confess every sin you have ever committed. You do not have to examine every nook and cranny of your life. You do not have to make sure you are willing to let God into each and every area, not missing one. Who could do that anyway? It is absurd, and so is this legalistic Lordship Salvation.

The Bible is clear that salvation is a gift. Gifts do not come with conditions. Gifts do not come with "sign on the dotted line" commitments. Those are purchases or contracts. They are not gifts. But salvation is a gift. Your part is to receive a gift. You will receive it after God touches your heart.

Everyone whom God elects will be saved. There will be no one in hell whom God wishes were in heaven. God hates sin and punishes sin. And when people are in hell, they are supposed to be there. God is not hoping you will make Him Lord of every area of your life. He is simply offering you a gift.

If you do not believe that, then He may not have touched your heart yet. Maybe you are not regenerated yet. Maybe He will touch you in your future. Maybe He will not. Some people do not make it to heaven. However, if any of this matters to you at all, it is **proof** that you are elect and that He is revealing the good news to you.

The good news is way easier than trying to be sure that you have made Jesus Lord of every area of your life. Instead, your eyes will be opened. All of a sudden, the gospel will make sense. You will receive a free gift with no strings attached. And then, with Christ in you, the hope of glory, you will progressively allow God to have more and more of your heart. Over time, you will be conformed to Christ's image. These legalists would have you learn all the possible lessons before you even come to Jesus. None of us can do that.

We come to Jesus as we are. He saves us, and then, over time, He gains more ground in our minds and lives as we become more and more sanctified. But that is never finished while we are on Earth. It is a process. And none of us are at the same place in that process.

Lordship Salvation removes that process from the Lord and puts it on us. We have to be willing in every area of our lives, or we are not saved. That is legalistic BS, and we stand against it.

Christian, remember your salvation experience. You brought nothing to the table. Maybe you believe some of this garbage teaching, and as a result, you are wondering if you have lost your salvation or if you ever were saved. That is the insidious nature of this false gospel. It makes people who have believed the true gospel doubt their salvation. That is not of God.

God wants you to have assurance of your salvation. Do not let anyone tell you that you are not committed enough and therefore not saved. No one has the right to say that about anyone. I do not have that right. Neither does John MacArthur nor any other teacher.

106

Lie #9 Christians Can Become So Holy In This Life That They No Longer Sin

Have you ever heard of the term *sinless perfection*? Lie number nine says that Christians can get to a place where they no longer sin. That is the lie of sinless perfection.

People who believe in sinless perfection do not like it when you use that term for their theology. But it is an accurate term. There are two flavors of this heresy:

1. From the moment a Christian is born again, they no longer sin.
2. As Christians progress in holiness, they can get to a point where they no longer sin.

One of the main verses that is used to support this concept is 1 John 5:18. Boy, the legalists love to twist the book of 1 John. Let's actually read verses 16 to 18:

If anyone sees his brother or sister committing a sin not leading to death, he shall ask and God will, for him, give life to those who commit sin not leading to death. There is sin leading to death; I am not saying that he should ask about that. All unrighteousness is sin, and there is sin not leading to death.

We know that no one who has been born of God sins; but He who was born of God keeps him, and the evil one does not touch him.[74]

If we take verse 18 out of context and use our black Bible highlighter on a bunch of verses surrounding it, verse 18 could seem to say that Christians do not sin.

So, let's put the cap back on our black Bible highlighter and take a look at the context. We do not have to look far. Check out verse 16:

If anyone sees his brother or sister committing sin

Let's just stop right there. That should settle it. This verse says the people sinning are our brothers and sisters. It says that we should pray for them when they are sinning. We should pray that God will give them life.

This cannot mean to pray for forgiveness because they are a brother or sister. They are already forgiven. What we are asking for is relief from the consequences of sin for our brothers and sisters. We would pray something like:

Lord, show them that what they are doing is wrong. By your life, help them to change their ways so they reap less earthly consequences.

Let's continue to look at verses 16 and 17. We cannot ignore the fact that John is talking about two kinds of sin here. The first is a sin not leading to death, and the second is a sin leading to death. What on Earth does that mean? Well, do we have any other place in Scripture where a certain sin is elevated to a level where it automatically leads to death? Is there an *unforgivable sin*? If you have been a Christian for any length of time, you have heard about the unforgivable sin. Let's look at Matthew 12:31:

"So I tell you, every sin and blasphemy can be forgiven— except blasphemy against the Holy Spirit, which will never be forgiven."[75]

People have talked about this forever. There are so many opinions about what "blasphemy against the Holy Spirit" means. First, let me tell you what it does not mean. Blasphemy against the Holy Spirit is not suicide, although many Christians believe it is. Suicide is a horrible thing that leaves a wake of pain and turmoil for generations. Suicide is self-murder. Murder is definitely a serious sin. But it is not unforgivable.

God forgives murder. He forgave Paul, who was at least an accessory to murder. Jesus asked the Father to forgive His murderers. So, if murdering the Son of God is not the unforgivable sin, then suicide cannot be either. So, what could be worse than murdering the Son of God? The answer is **unbelief**.

Now you may say, how can unbelief be worse than murder? Let me explain. Unbelief says that God is a liar. God says that Jesus is the only way. If you do not believe that, you are calling God a liar. More specifically, you are calling the Holy Spirit a liar. The Holy Spirit inspired the Scriptures. The main way that God communicates with the human race is through the Holy Spirit. Remember, the Holy Spirit convicts unbelievers of sin.

Therefore, someone who remains in unbelief until they die has committed a sin that is not forgivable because they have called the One Who offers forgiveness a liar, and they do not believe that they have any need of Him. That is blasphemy. Living your entire life rejecting Jesus is the unforgivable sin. That is the sin that leads to spiritual death. Everyone in hell will have committed the unforgivable sin. They have gone to their deaths calling God a liar.

Once we see the distinction between the two kinds of sin in verses 16 and 17, verse 18 starts to make sense. Verse 18 cannot mean that Christians never sin because verse 16 comes right out and contradicts it.

Verse 16 also says that there is a sin leading to death. What is that sin? It is the sin of unbelief. And guess what! All of your praying for an unbeliever will not make that unbeliever a believer. God has to do that. And He has decided this before the foundation of the world. So, John is not necessarily saying here that you cannot pray for sinners. He may be saying that you may not get the answer you want.

We should pray for sinning Christians (which all of us are). They are His. But, if you do not know that they are His, your prayer may not be answered the way you want.

It is possible that John is saying that you may not get the answer you expect if you pray for God to forgive the unforgivable sin, which is lifelong unbelief. That makes sense, right? Can we find out more about what verse 18 means?

Well, let's look at something else it does not mean. Many popular theologians explain this verse in a certain manner, and I just have to disagree. They say that the verse means no one who is born of God *makes a practice of sinning*. The New Living Translation even uses that exact phrase. But is that what the verse says? To find out, we will have to look at the Greek word for *sin* in this verse.

The word is *hamartano*, which means:

to miss the mark; to go toward the wrong finish line in a race

Verbs in Greek have four characteristics. Actually, verbs in all languages have these characteristics. But in English, we use extra words to show these characteristics. For example, consider the sentence:

If I make it to tomorrow, I will have lasted five days on this diet.

The verb "to last" does not tell the whole story in its infinitive form. We have added the words "*will have*". In many other languages, these extra words that we need in English to convey tense are just built into the verb. The ending of the verb changes, and that tells you all you need to know. If you have ever studied a foreign language, especially a Latin-based language, you understand this.

The four characteristics of Greek verbs are person, voice, tense, and mood. Verse 18 says:

We know that no one who has been born of God sins.

The word "sins" (*hamartano*) is in the third person, active voice, present tense, and indicative mood. What does all that mean? You will never believe it! It means that the proper translation of this verse is:

We know that no one who has been born of God sins.

That is exactly what the verse says. Yet many Bible teachers try to refute sinless perfection, which they should, by adding to this verse the concept of "*making a practice of sinning.*" But that is not what this verse says.

In Greek, there is no other way to say "*no one who is born of God sins.*" But there are other ways to say, "*no one who is born of God makes a practice of sinning.*" There are words and tenses in Greek for "*makes a practice of sinning.*" Why did John not use that language? Because he said exactly what he wanted to say. No one who is born of God sins.

I have been born again for almost four decades, and I am so grateful that God has kept me all of this time. I do not feel holier now than I did when I first got saved. In fact, I feel less holy. I agree with Paul in Romans 7. I am a wretched man. I still sin. Therefore, I am either not saved, or sinless perfection is wrong.

And instead of refuting sinless perfection, those who say that this means *continually practicing* sin are actually unknowingly reinforcing sinless perfection. They have just created a special class of people who accidentally sin but do not make a practice of it. Well, I have not gone one day in my life without sinning. I think that means I have made a practice of sinning.

Therefore, if the legalistic interpretation of the verse is correct, I am not a Christian. But if it just means what it seems to say - that no one who is born of God sins at all, ever again - that does not seem to jive with many other verses.

For example, James 3:2 says:

Indeed, we all make many mistakes. For if we could control our tongues, we would be perfect and could also control ourselves in every other way.[76]

Another compelling example that Christians still sin is Philippians 3:12. Paul says:

I don't mean to say that I have already achieved these things or that I have already reached perfection. But I press on to possess that perfection for which Christ Jesus first possessed me.[77]

Paul clearly says here that he has not reached perfection. Another great example from Paul is when he is instructing Timothy, a young church leader that Paul mentored. In 1 Timothy 1:15, Paul says:

This is a trustworthy saying, and everyone should accept it: "Christ Jesus came into the world to save sinners"—and I am the worst of them all.[78]

Paul does not say, "*and I **was** the worst of them all.*" He uses the present tense.

Just in case you still do not believe that Christians sin, I am going to give you one more verse. Paul cries out in Romans 7:24:

Oh, what a miserable person I am! Who will free me from this life that is dominated by sin and death?[79]

I believe the verses above show that Christians still sin after salvation. But 1 John 5:18 seems to say that Christians do not sin. How do we reconcile all of these verses?

1 John 5:18 cannot mean that Christians never, ever sin after salvation. There are too many verses that say they do. And if we are honest, we know we still sin. So, what could it mean?

Let's look at the context. We cannot ignore verses 16 and 17, which talk about two kinds of sin. By looking at the context, we see the meaning and intention of this verse: that Christians cannot commit the sin leading to death.

There is no other way to interpret this Scripture in light of all the other verses that show Christians continue to sin. If this verse means that Christians never sin, consider these necessary implications. Twenty-four hours a day, seven days a week, from the moment you got saved until you die:

- Every word you say has to be perfect.
- Every thought you think has to be perfect.
- Every action you do has to be perfect.
- All of your motives and intentions must be perfect.

- You must be perfect at loving God with all of your heart, soul, mind, and strength.

- You must be perfect at loving your neighbor as much and in the same way as you love yourself.

- You must always have faith in every situation because whatsoever is not of faith is sin.

- You must take up your cross every day and follow Jesus.

- You must trust in the Lord with all of your heart.

- You must never lean on your own understanding.

- You must acknowledge God in all of your ways.

Listen, I could go on forever, but I think you get the point. Anyone who tells you they do not sin is a liar. So, what does all this mean?

If we still sin, do those sins need to be forgiven each time they are committed? This may shock you, but the answer is no. I know that goes against much of the teaching that is out there. But there are also many teachers that agree with what I am about to say.

There is no re-forgiveness. You were forgiven when Jesus died. You accepted that forgiveness when you got saved. Forgiveness is a settled issue. You do not get forgiven of your sins by confessing them to Jesus after your Christian. Now, talking to Jesus and agreeing with Him about your sin is a great thing to do. That is what the word confess means. Confess means to *say with* or to *agree with* someone. So, to agree with God about your sin is a good thing. And talking to God about your struggles is what we are supposed to do.

But talking to God about the sin you committed yesterday as a Christian does not get you forgiven. Talking to God is always a good thing to do. However, there is no process of penance, conditional forgiveness, or ongoing confession of each sin for the purpose of being forgiven. These concepts are not scriptural.

Now, you may say, "Rick, what is your point? Why even have a chapter like this?" The reason is that the gospel is at stake. There is a massive move in contemporary Christianity toward legalism and away from the gospel of grace. And it is only the legalist who would tell you that you can get to a point where you no longer sin. Have you ever noticed that the ones who believe in sinless perfection always tell you that they have arrived at that point? They remind me of the rich young ruler, who thought he kept the whole law. They are never honest like Paul. Paul said he had not arrived. Paul said that he was a wretched man. Paul said he could not do the right thing, and he sinned all the time. Paul definitely did not teach sinless perfection.

Why is this lie so destructive? There are two reasons.

The first reason is that this bad doctrine causes Christians to doubt their salvation. In that sense, it causes the same damage as Lordship Salvation. We may think, "If Christians never sin, but I do, I must not be a Christian."

Anyone who is honest would conclude, if this doctrine is correct, that they are not saved.

The second reason this lie is so destructive is that it makes Christians look ridiculous to the world. Now, I understand that the gospel is foolishness to the flesh, but that is not what I mean. Unbelievers see our sin. Then they hear us say that we do not have any sin. And they say, "Liar! Hypocrite!" And they are correct.

Listen, dear Christian, to the truth of Scripture. Jesus has taken His place as our Advocate and Intercessor. He is our Lawyer in heaven, reminding God that we are in Christ. The Bible says that the devil is the accuser of the brethren. Satan is the prosecutor, pointing out our sins to the Father. Jesus is our defense attorney, objecting every time an accusation is brought against us, saying, "Objection! This sin is covered because I paid for it. This Christian is hidden in Me." You have nothing to do or say in this courtroom. Your Advocate, your Lawyer, speaks on your behalf.

I do not have to convince you that you still sin. Even if you say you believe in sinless perfection, deep down, you know better. If you believe in sinless perfection, either you are denying what you know to be true, or you are deceived and not a Christian. I know that sounds harsh, but it is the harsh truth. If you are trusting in the fact that you no longer sin, you have not accepted the true gospel.

Maybe this doctrine of sinless perfection has caused you to think incorrectly. That is the danger of this doctrine. It causes born-again, blood-washed Christians to wonder if they are genuine Christians. If that is you, you need to reject this lie from the devil. If you have accepted the free gift of salvation, if you believe in your heart and confess with your mouth, you are a Christian. You will sin until you die because that is how long you will still have a flesh with which to contend. However, you are already seen as perfect before God. You are viewed as someone who exhibits sinless perfection. But it is not because you do not sin. It is because your sins are gone. They are wiped away. They are forgiven. They are not on your account. In God's eyes, you are as sinless as Jesus.

The doctrine that Christians can become so holy in this life that they no longer sin is a stinking lie. And like all lies, it is dangerous because it leads people away from the truth. The truth is that we all struggle in this life. Christians and non-Christians alike sin. The difference between the two groups is that non-Christians are committing the sin of unbelief, which, if they die in that sin, will send them to hell. On the other hand, all of a Christian's sins - past, present, and future - are forgiven. This is the good news. This is the gospel.

Lie #10 It Is Not God's Will For Christians To Suffer

We have arrived at lie number ten. This list was not arranged in any particular order. But perhaps God wanted this one for last because suffering seems to be ramping up in our world. Certainly, terrorism, COVID, rioting, unemployment, and many other trials seem to be besieging us currently.

Reformed theologians talk about two different aspects of the will of God. They distinguish between the *decretive will* of God and the *preceptive will* of God. An easy way to distinguish one from another is to look at the roots of each of these words. The root of decretive is *decree*. The root of preceptive is *precept*.

First, let's discuss God's decretive will. When God said, "Let there be light," He decreed that there would be light, and it happened. Light had no choice. God's will was for there to be light, and there was light. God's decretive will is secret to us. We do not know it and cannot presume to know it. He is sovereign. No person has this power of will. No man is guaranteed that, by willing something, it will come to pass. This is what is so wrong with the "Christian" concepts of positive confession and speaking things into being. We do not have the power of a decretive will.

When God says, "Do not murder," He is giving us a statement of *preceptive* will. In other words, God stating a precept does not mean He forces everyone to obey it. God's decretive will always happens. It always comes to pass. God's preceptive will lays out precepts and consequences for obeying or disobeying those precepts.

We have to be careful, however, not to make too much of a difference between these two types of God's will. God's preceptive will is just as holy and right as His decretive will. God's precepts are as true as His decrees. His precepts are based on His moral law, which is absolutely true. The difference is whether the recipient has a choice. The light had no choice when God said let there be light. But humans have a choice when God says not to bear false witness.

In the context of suffering, it is accurate to say that God's preceptive will is that He does not want Christians to suffer. Yet, His sovereignty decrees that they will.

If there were no distinction between these two aspects of God's will, consider the ramifications. If "Let there be light" was a statement of God's preceptive will, then light could have disobeyed. That is not possible. And if "thou shalt not bear false witness" came from God's decretive will, then no one would ever lie. Hopefully, that makes sense.

So then, why do Christians suffer? There are three types of suffering that Christians endure. The first is general suffering, which is the consequence of the fall of the human race. Genesis 3:16-19 says:

Then he said to the woman, "I will sharpen the pain of your pregnancy, and in pain you will give birth. And you will desire to control your husband, but he will rule over you."

And to the man he said, "Since you listened to your wife and ate from the tree whose fruit I commanded you not to eat, the ground is cursed because of you.

All your life you will struggle to scratch a living from it. It will grow thorns and thistles for you, though you will eat of its grains.

By the sweat of your brow will you have food to eat until you return to the ground from which you were made.

For you were made from dust, and to dust you will return."[80]

This type of suffering is common to all of us. Our years on Earth are numbered. Psalm 90:10 tells us that approximately seventy to eighty years are given to us. That verse also says that even the best years we have are filled with pain and trouble. Soon they disappear, and we fly away. That is the general suffering that is common to humans.

The second type of suffering happens because of bad choices. If you drink too much, your liver will suffer. If you do not take care of your money, you will come to poverty. If you rob a bank, you could go to jail or even get shot. Even if you are a Christian, these things can happen to you. Disobey God's preceptive will, and there will be consequences.

The third type is **suffering for Christ**. Check out Romans 8:17-18:

And since we are his children, we are his heirs. In fact, together with Christ we are heirs of God's glory. But if we are to share his glory, we must also share his suffering.

Yet what we suffer now is nothing compared to the glory he will reveal to us later.[81]

In John 15:18-21, Jesus said:

If the world hates you, remember that it hated me first. The world would love you as one of its own if you belonged to it, but you are no longer part of the world. I chose you to come out of the world, so it hates you. Do you remember what I told you? 'A slave is not greater than the master.' Since they persecuted me, naturally they will persecute you. And if they had listened to me, they would listen to you. They will do all this to you because of me, for they have rejected the one who sent me.[82]

Now, this is Jesus speaking. How can anyone argue with this verse? Here are some examples of suffering for Christ that Christians have endured. First, Brian Bell notes in his commentary on the Bible:

At the Nicene Council, an important church meeting in the 4th century A.D., of the three hundred and eighteen delegates attending, fewer than 12 had not lost an eye or lost a hand or did not limp on a leg lamed by torture for their Christian faith.[83]

Christians have always suffered on Earth. Let's take a look at the Apostles. How did the Apostles die?

Well, Paul was beheaded in 66 A.D. Peter was crucified upside down around the same time. Thomas was speared by four soldiers. Andrew was crucified in Greece. Philip was put to death by the Roman Proconsul after he converted the Proconsul's wife. Matthew was stabbed to death in Ethiopia. James was stoned and clubbed to death. Simon the Zealot was killed after refusing to sacrifice to the sun god. Matthias, Judas's replacement, was burned at the stake in Syria. John, the only Apostle to die a natural death, was boiled in oil and survived. He was then exiled to an island called Patmos.

But Christian persecution did not stop with the Apostles. Early Christians were fed to lions as sport in front of massive crowds. Sometimes they were forced to fight gladiators. That seldom went well for the Christian.

What about Christians today? Are Christians suffering today? Angelus News says that two hundred and sixty million Christians are facing persecution around the world. The number one country that persecutes Christians is North Korea. They have three hundred thousand Christians out of a population of twenty-five million. If Christians are discovered in North Korea, the government either deports them to a labor camp or kills them on the spot. Following North Korea are Afghanistan, Somalia, Libya, Pakistan, Eritrea, Sudan, Yemen, Iran, and India. Those are the top 10 countries that persecute Christians. [84]

China is number twenty-three on the list. In 2018, 793 churches were attacked by the Chinese government. In 2020, the estimate is that 5,576 churches will have been attacked in China alone. It is going to get much worse.[85]

Now, so far, you might be saying to yourself, "This chapter is a big fat downer," and I can understand that. But I would like to conclude this chapter with a bit more of a focus on the benefits of suffering.

Suffering has many benefits for a Christian. Suffering leads to eternal glory. Romans 8:18 says:

Yet what we suffer now is nothing compared to the glory he will reveal to us later.[86]

We have no idea what awaits us. Amazing glory with Jesus will be our eternal future. We will not even remember this suffering.

In Luke 18:29, Jesus gives us an amazing promise:

"Yes," Jesus replied, "and I assure you that everyone who has given up house or wife or brothers or parents or children, for the sake of the Kingdom of God, will be repaid many times over in this life, and will have eternal life in the world to come."[87]

Jesus promises that our suffering will not be in vain.

Another benefit of suffering is that it can enable you to transmit comfort to others in their time of suffering. We read in 2 Corinthians 1:3-4:

All praise to God, the Father of our Lord Jesus Christ. God is our merciful Father and the source of all comfort. He comforts us in all our troubles so that we can comfort others. When they are troubled, we will be able to give them the same comfort God has given us.[88]

When we suffer, we are able to relate to others who suffer, and we can help them.

A third benefit is that suffering teaches us to persevere and helps us grow up. Listen to what the brother of Jesus says about suffering in James 1:2-4:

Dear brothers and sisters, when troubles of any kind come your way, consider it an opportunity for great joy. For you know that when your faith is tested, your endurance has a chance to grow. So let it grow, for when your endurance is fully developed, you will be perfect and complete, needing nothing.[89]

God definitely uses suffering for our good. Let's look at some of God's promises for us when we suffer. 1 Peter 3:14 says this:

But even if you suffer for doing what is right, God will reward you for it. So don't worry or be afraid of their threats.[90]

That is a good word for us, isn't it? Here is another. 1 Peter 4:1:

So then, since Christ suffered physical pain, you must arm yourselves with the same attitude he had, and be ready to suffer, too. For if you have suffered physically for Christ, you have finished with sin.[91]

But God is not going to leave us without help or hope when we suffer. Look at 1 Peter 5:10:

In his kindness God called you to share in his eternal glory by means of Christ Jesus. So after you have suffered a little while, he will restore, support, and strengthen you, and he will place you on a firm foundation.[92]

God says we are going to suffer, but He does not leave us alone in the suffering. Life on this side of heaven is full of suffering, but it is also full of joy. The insidiousness of this lie - that it is not God's will for Christians to suffer - is that it heaps guilt on the sufferers. In other words, suffering is your own fault, and God is not going to help you. Isn't legalism great? Legalism is like throwing an anchor instead of a life preserver to a drowning person.

It is not true that God only helps you when you are suffering for Him. God will help you even if the suffering is a consequence of your own sin. I know this because of Romans 8:28:

And we know that God causes everything to work together for the good of those who love God and are called according to his purpose for them.[27]

Without human suffering, we would not know God's deliverance. Without the suffering of a Christian, growth would not happen in this life. You know this. Growth comes through pain.

Christian, if you are suffering right now, no matter what the reason, we can pray that God will use your suffering for your good and His glory, even if you are suffering for your own mistakes. God can and will still use this for our good.

And if you are not a Christian, God may be allowing suffering in your life for the same reason He allows it in a Christian's life - to call us to draw us closer to Him.

But if you ignore this call, your suffering may get worse. And if you ignore it permanently, your suffering will be permanent. Give your life to Christ. He will give your suffering purpose.

Some of the most altruistic and empathetic people are those who have suffered horribly. Maybe God wants to transform you into that type of person, but you must first confess that much of your suffering is because of your sin, and you must receive forgiveness for that sin.

The thought that it is not God's will for Christians to suffer is a stinking lie. Jesus suffered horribly, and He told us that a servant is not greater than his master. Without suffering, we would be robbed of the experience of God's deliverance, and we would be robbed of opportunities to grow. Christians suffer, and God is good. That is the reality of the Christian life.

Conclusion

My purpose in this book was not to be insulting, fault-finding, nor critical of anyone's personal life. The purpose was to be used by God to help set people free from legalism. I pray that will happen. That would be my greatest joy.

I do not claim to have perfect doctrine. I am constantly learning. Therefore, I am open to correction, as we all should be. And, possibly, God will use this book for the purpose of correction. I wish no ill will to anyone who does not agree with what I have written. Nor do I wish any to those who teach the errors outlined in this book.

I simply pray that, as Jesus comes into better focus in our lives, we will look away from ourselves and learn to trust completely in the love and grace of Jesus. The gospel really is good news. Anything that diminishes that good news is a lie.

Thank you for taking the time to read this book to the end. I hope your faith is better for it. I give God credit for any truth in this book, and I pray that anything else would just fall away.

I will close with the same wish for you that Peter wishes for us.

May God give you more and more grace and peace as you grow in your knowledge of God and Jesus, our Lord.

130

Acknowledgments

There are so many people to thank for helping me. Some have helped directly with this project, and some have helped me understand what has been taught here.

I will start with the second category first. I want to express my gratitude to the following teachers of sound doctrine:

Tullian Tchividjian
Chuck Swindoll
James White
Andrew Farley

Now, I'd like to get a bit more personal.

Kim White – my wife, and Chief Encouragement Officer of Grace Online Church

Thank you for everything you do, and particularly for your help with this book. You help me express ideas in ways that make more sense, and you help me to not write the wrong things. Everyone reading this book should thank you for that. I love you more than I can say.

Loel Passe – my best friend and partner in ministry
Brother, this book would not have been completed without your encouragement, support, and input. Thank you for the kind words in the foreword.

I would also like to thank the following people, who helped with proofreading, encouragement, insight, and prayer:

Michael Evans
Don St. George
Rick Bailey
Sammy Oriti
Zach White
Baylee White
Joe Courrege

I would like to thank God, Who never condemns me, never gives up on me, and continues to show me the lies that I so readily believe. All of my trust is in You, Lord. Eternity will not be enough time to thank You for what You have done.

Finally, I would like to thank you, the reader, for purchasing this book and making it to the end. If this has caused you to think, I have been successful, even if you disagree with me.

I wish you all grace and peace from the only One Who can provide those gifts. Writing this book has given me a clearer picture of what God has accomplished on my behalf. I pray that reading it will have done the same for you.

Works Cited

[1] John 8:32 NLT: Then you will know the truth, and the truth will https://biblehub.com/john/8-32.htm

[2] 2 Timothy 4:2-5 - NLT - Preach the word of God.... https://www.biblestudytools.com/nlt/2-timothy/passage/?q=2-timothy+4:2-5

[3] John 15:16 NLT: You didn't choose me. I chose https://www.bible.com/bible/116/JHN.15.16.nlt

[4] Romans 9:18 NLT: So you see, God chooses… https://biblehub.com/nlt/romans/9-18.htm

[5] Romans 9:20-24 NLT: When a potter makes jars https://biblehub.com/nlt/romans/9-20.htm

[6] Genesis 15:17 NLT: After the sun went down and.... https://biblehub.com/nlt/genesis/15-17.htm

[7] Ephesians 2:8-9 NLT: God saved you by his .... https://www.biblegateway.com/passage/?search=Ephesians%202:8-9&version=NLT

[8] John 6:35-37 NLT: Jesus replied, "I am the bread.... https://www.biblegateway.com/passage/?search=John+6%3A35-40&version=NLT

[9] Revelation 22:17 NLT: The Spirit and the bride https://www.bible.com/bible/116/REV.22.17.nlt

[10] John 10:27-29 NLT: My sheep listen to my ....
https://www.biblegateway.com/passage/?search=Jo
hn%2010:27-29&version=NLT

[11] Romans 3:10 NLT: As it is written: "There is no ....
https://biblehub.com/romans/3-10.htm

[12] 1 Corinthians 2:14 NLT: But people who aren't ....
https://biblehub.com/nlt/1_corinthians/2-14.htm

[13] Galatians 3:1-5 NLT: Oh, foolish
Galatians!....
https://www.bible.com/bible/116/gal.3.1-5.nlt

[14] Galatians 3:4 NLT: Have you experienced....
https://biblehub.com/nlt/galatians/3-4.htm

[15] Romans 8:35-40 NLT: Can anything ever ....
https://www.biblegateway.com/passage/?search=Ro
mans%208:35-40&version=NLT

[16] Philippians 1:6 NLT: And I am certain that God, ...
https://biblehub.com/nlt/philippians/1-6.htm

[17] 1 Peter 1:4-5 NLT: and we have a
priceless…https://www.biblegateway.com/passage/?
search=1+Peter+1%3A4-5&version=NLT

[18] Hebrews 6:4-6: So let us stop going over basic ....
https://www.biblegateway.com/passage/?search=He
brews+6%3A4-6&version=NLT

[19] Matthew 7:21-24: "Not everyone who calls out...
https://www.bible.com/bible/116/MAT.7.13-14,21-24.NLT

[20] John 6:40 NLT: For it is my Father's will that all....
https://www.biblegateway.com/passage/?search=John+6%3A40&version=NLT

[21] Matthew 7:23 NLT: "Get away from me ....
https://www.biblegateway.com/passage/?search=Matthew%207%3A21-27&version=NLT

[22] Psalm 103:12 NLT: He has removed our sins as...
https://classic.biblegateway.com/passage/?search=Psalm+103%3A12&version=NLT

[23] Revelation 16 NLT: Then I heard a mighty....
https://www.biblegateway.com/passage/?search=Revelation%2016&version=NLT

[24] 2 Corinthians 5:21 NLT: For God made Christ...
https://www.biblehub.com/nlt/2_corinthians/5-21.htm

[25] 1 Peter 2:24 NLT: - He personally carried our ...
https://www.biblegateway.com/passage/?search=1%20Peter%202:24&version=NLT

[26] Galatians 3:10 NLT: - But those who depend on ....
https://www.biblegateway.com/passage/?search=Galatians+3%3A10&version=NLT

[27] Romans 8:28 NLT: And we know that God....
https://www.biblehub.com/nlt/romans/8-28.htm

[28] Does God get disappointed with us? - Religion News Service.
https://religionnews.com/2013/06/21/does-god-get-disappointed-with-us/

[29] MacArthur, John F. (2009-05-26). The Gospel According to Jesus: What Is Authentic Faith? Zondervan. ePub Edition.

[30] Romans 10:9-10 NLT: If you openly declare....
https://www.bible.com/bible/116/ROM.10.9-13.nlt

[31] Isaiah 41:21-23 NLT: "Present the case for your....
https://www.bible.com/bible/116/ISA.41.21-23.nlt

[32] Isaiah 42:8-9 NLT: I am the LORD; that is ....
https://biblehub.com/isaiah/42-8.htm

[33] Ephesians 1:3-5 NLT: All praise to God, the ....
https://www.biblestudytools.com/nlt/ephesians/passage/?q=ephesians+1:3-5

[34] Galatians 2:20 NLT: I have been crucified with...
https://biblehub.com/galatians/2-20.htm

[35] Ephesians 1:5 NLT: God decided in advance to...
https://www.bible.com/bible/116/EPH.1.5.nlt

[36] Luke 12:32 NLT: So don't be afraid, little flock…
https://www.bible.com/bible/116/luk.12.32

[37] Ephesians 2:6 NLT: For he raised us from the ....
https://www.biblegateway.com/passage/?search=Ephesians+2%3A6&version=NLT

[38] John 16:8 NLT: But in fact, it is best for you that...
https://www.biblegateway.com/passage/?search=John+16%3A7-11&version=NLT

[39] Romans 10:9-10 NLT: If you openly declare that ...
https://www.bible.com/bible/116/ROM.10.9-10.nlt

[40] Romans 1:4 NLT: and he was shown to be the....
https://biblehub.com/nlt/romans/1-4.htm

[41] 1 Corinthians 15:17 NLT: And if Christ has not ...
https://www.biblegateway.com/passage/?search=1+corinthians+15%3A17&version=NLT

[42] 1 John 1:9 NLT: But if we confess our sins...
https://www.biblegateway.com/passage/?search=1+John+1%3A9&version=NLT

[43] 1 John 1:8 NLT: But if we confess our sins...
https://www.biblegateway.com/passage/?search=1+John+1%3A8&version=NLT

[44] James 2:10 NLT: For the person who keeps...
https://www.biblegateway.com/passage/?search=james+2%3A10&version=NLT

[45] John 1:16 NLT - From his abundance we ....
https://www.biblegateway.com/passage/?search=Jo
hn+1:16&version=NLT

[47] James 4:6 NLT -And he gives grace....
https://www.biblegateway.com/passage/?search=Ja
mes+4%3A6&version=NLT

[48]Luke 18:9-14 NLT - Then Jesus told this story....
https://www.bible.com/bible/116/LUK.18.9-14.nlt

[49] Romans 5:20 Parallel: Moreover the law entered....
https://biblehub.com/parallel/romans/5-20.htm

[50] Romans 8:33-34 NLT -Who dares accuse us....
https://www.biblegateway.com/passage/?search=Ro
mans+8%3A33-34&version=NLT

[51] Mark 1:4 NLT - John the Baptist appeared in the....
https://www.biblehub.com/mark/1-4.htm

[52] Mark 1:14-15 KJV - Now after that John was ....
https://www.bible.com/bible/1/MRK.1.14-15.kjv

[53] John 20:31 NLV -But these are written ....
https://www.biblegateway.com/verse/en/John%2020
%3A31

[54] 1 Peter 1:2-4 NLT - God the Father knew you ....
https://www.biblegateway.com/passage/?search=1+
Peter+1%3A2-4&version=NLT

55 1 Corinthians 2:14 NLT - But people who aren't ....
https://www.bible.com/bible/116/1CO.2.14.nlt

56 2 Timothy 2:24-26 NLT - And a servant of the ....
https://www.biblegateway.com/passage/?search=2+
Timothy+2%3A24-26+&version=NLT

57 Acts 11:18 NLT - When the others heard this ....
https://www.biblegateway.com/passage/?search=act
s+11%3A18&version=NLT

58 Acts 13:48 - NLT - When the Gentiles heard ....
https://www.biblestudytools.com/nlt/acts/13-48.html

59 Ezekiel 36:26 NLT - I will give you a new heart ....
https://www.biblehub.com/ezekiel/36-26.htm

60 Ephesians 2:8-9 NLT - God saved you by his ....
https://www.biblegateway.com/passage/?search=Ep
hesians%202:8-9&version=NLT

61 Romans 3:9-20 NLT - Well then, should we ....
https://www.bible.com/bible/116/ROM.3.9-20.nlt

62 Isaiah 64:6 NLT - We are all infected and ....
https://www.bible.com/bible/116/ISA.64.6.nlt

63 1 John 1:5 NLT - This is the message we heard ....
https://biblehub.com/nlt/1_john/1-5.htm

64 Acts 5:1-11 NLT - But there was a certain ....
https://www.biblegateway.com/passage/?search=Act
s+5%3A1-11&version=NLT

[65] Isaiah 59:2 NLT - It's your sins that have cut ....
https://www.biblegateway.com/passage/?search=Isaiah+59%3A2&version=NLT

[66] Matthew 25:46 NLT - And they will go away ....
https://www.biblehub.com/matthew/25-46.htm

[67] Matthew 10:28 Do not be afraid of those who ....
https://biblehub.com/matthew/10-28.htm

[68] Mark 9:47-48 NLT - And if your eye causes ....
https://www.biblegateway.com/passage/?search=Mark+9%3A47-48&version=NLT

[69] Revelation 14:9-11 NLT - Then a third angel ....
https://www.biblegateway.com/passage/?search=Revelation+14%3A9-11&version=NLT

[70] Romans 9:18-21 NLT - So you see, God....
https://www.biblegateway.com/passage/?search=romans+9%3A18-21+&version=NLT

[71] Mark 10:17-22 - NLT - As Jesus was starting ....
https://www.biblestudytools.com/nlt/mark/passage/?q=mark+10:17-22

[72] Romans 3:20 NLT - For no one can ever be ....
https://www.biblegateway.com/passage/?search=Romans+3%3A20&version=NLT

[73] Luke 10:25-30 NLT - One day an expert ....
https://www.bible.com/bible/116/LUK.10.25-30.NLT

74 1 John 5:16-18 NASB - If anyone sees his....
https://www.biblegateway.com/passage/?search=1J
ohn+5%3A16-18+&version=NASB

75 Matthew 12:31 NLT - "So I tell you, every ....
https://www.biblegateway.com/passage/?search=Ma
tthew+12%3A31&version=NLT

76 James 3:2 NLT - Indeed, we all make many ....
https://www.biblegateway.com/passage/?search=Ja
mes+3%3A2&version=NLT

77 Philippians 3:12 NLT: I don't mean to say that I....
https://www.biblehub.com/nlt/philippians/3-12.htm

78 1 Timothy 1:15 NLT - This is a trustworthy ....
https://www.biblegateway.com/passage/?search=1+
Timothy+1%3A15&version=NLT

79 Romans 7:24-25 NLT - Oh, what a miserable....
https://www.biblegateway.com/passage/?search=Ro
mans+7%3A24-25&version=NLT

80 Genesis 3:16-19 NLT - Then he said to the....
https://www.biblegateway.com/passage/?search=Ge
nesis+3%3A16-19&version=NLT

81 Romans 8:17-18 NLT - And since we are his ....
https://www.biblegateway.com/passage/?search=Ro
mans+8%3A17-18+&version=NLT

[82] John 15:18-21 NLT - *If the world hates you...*
https://www.biblegateway.com/passage/?search=John+15%3A18-21+&version=NLT

[83] Romans 8 - Brian Bell Commentary on the Bible -
https://www.studylight.org/commentaries/eng/cbb/romans-8.html

[84] The Top 10 Countries for the Persecution of Christians (2019)
https://www.webtruth.org/cultural-issues/the-top-10-countries-in-the-world-for-persecution-of-christians-2019/

[85] Christian Headlines - China Persecuted 5,576 ....
https://www.christianheadlines.com/contributors/michael-foust/china-persecuted-5576-churches-in-2019-climbs-to-23-on-worst-persecutors-list.html

[86] Romans 8:18 NLT - Yet what we suffer now is ....
https://biblehub.com/nlt/romans/8-18.htm

[87] Luke 18:29 NLT - "Yes," Jesus replied, "and ....
https://biblehub.com/nlt/luke/18-29.htm

[88] 2 Corinthians 1:4 NLT – All praise to God ....
https://www.biblegateway.com/passage/?search=2+Corinthians+1%3A3-4&version=NLT

[89] James 1:2-4 Dear brothers and sisters, when ....
https://www.bible.com/bible/116/JAS.1.2-4.nlt

[90] 1 Peter 3:14 NLT - But even if you suffer for ....
https://www.biblegateway.com/passage/?search=1+Peter+3%3A14&version=NLT

[91] 1 Peter 4:1 NLT - So then, since Christ suffered....
https://biblehub.com/nlt/1_peter/4-1.htm

[92] 1 Peter 5:10 NLT - In his kindness God called ....
https://biblehub.com/nlt/1_peter/5-10.htm

In "The Top 10 Stinking Lies From The Pulpit," Pastor Rick White challenges ten beliefs that are taught in many churches today. Rick uses an abundance of verses to debunk these Christian myths that have caused the faith of many to be shipwrecked. Your theological notions very well may be challenged while reading. That is the express purpose of this book - to shed the light of Scripture on some very common false teachings. With humility and humor, Rick leaves you with confidence in the grace of God. If you trust in your own human nature to be good and holy, this book will challenge you. But, if you read to the end, you may be set free from legalism and religion, and you will see the Amazing Grace of God in a new way. Are you up for the challenge?

More information is available at
www.graceonlinechurch.org
or
facebook.com/thegraceonlinechurch.

To support this ministry, please visit
www.patreon.com/graceonlinechurch.

Made in the USA
Columbia, SC
23 August 2021

44135077R00083